THE GOD OF WELCOMES

Peter Ward CSsR

The God of Welcomes

For those who have almost given up

the columba press

First published, 1996, by
the columba press
55A Spruce Avenue, Stillorgan Industrial Park,
Blackrock, Co Dublin
Reprinted 1997

Cover by Bill Bolger
Cover photograph by courtesy of
The Office of Public Works, Dublin
Origination by The Columba Press
Printed in Ireland by e-print, Dublin

ISBN 1 85607 168 5

Contents

I fled him down the nights and down the days;
I fled him down the arches of the years;
I fled him down the labyrinthine ways
of my own mind: and in the mist of tears
I hid from him.

Francis Thompson, *The Hound of Heaven*

PART I

The way God leads us into transformation

CHAPTER 1

The beginning of the spiritual life

For years I wondered what the spiritual life was all about. I studied. I made retreats. I tried to do what others suggested and what I read in books. Yet nothing seemed to work. I had almost given up.

However, one day when I was in my mid-thirties, I met a Brother in Calcutta and I knew that something new had come into my life. He spoke of God and of prayer. But he spoke of them in a way that I had been waiting for for years. Those were the things I had been interested in for a long time, yet nothing seemed to click until that meeting.

That was the beginning of a development that started in me and has been going on ever since. When I look back on it now I can see a very definite process. Indeed, I can trace it step by step. But that process is not peculiar to me. It is the same process that goes on in all of us.

In many years of doing of spiritual direction, I have been listening to what others have to say about their relationship with God and with other people. I have noticed the same process going on in them. Though we are all different in so many ways, there seems to be the same pattern in the story of each one of us. So I would like to share my ideas with those who are interested. Since there is one experience of the spiritual life that I know best of all, and that is my own, I will take that as the basis of what I want to say.

My own feeble efforts
It was not that I had been constantly thinking about the spiritual

life when I was young. Far from it. After my novitiate, when I was a clerical student in Galway, the thought of the spiritual life *did* keep turning up from time to time. During retreats, my interest would be rekindled. I used ask myself how I could advance. I must have had a vague wish to get God more into my life, though I suppose everyone has that. And, also, I wanted to be better! If I were honest, I suppose that meant that I would have liked to cut a better figure before others! I would have liked to do things that would have caused admiration among my confrères. But then, after the retreat, the desire would gradually fade away again. Other more immediate interests took its place.

However, that is not surprising, as there was a lot of competition at different stages in my life. Especially as a student, I was preocupied with many things. There were my studies, my work about the house, my relationships with others, games, acting in plays, the books I was reading. Even the lives of the saints, which we read a lot in those days, only discouraged me.

Eventually, I began to think that getting any better or holier was not really for me. I suppose when it is obvious that something is beyond us, most of us ask, despairingly, does it matter anyway? And yet it did. At least from time to time it did seem important to me. Besides, a deep longing persisted. Though I had studied what we used to call Ascetical Theology, I had no idea what the spiritual life really was. Nor had I any idea what I was looking for. That is until things began to happen.

Two experiences
Unexpectedly, I had what could only be called an experience of God. It was not that I saw anything or heard anything. It was just that God seemed close. It was then I came to this seemingly obvious conclusion: the spiritual life had something to do with God. That I always kind of expected, but when it happened it was not in the way I had imagined.

Then I went through the opposite experience – a failure. For me it was devastating. It was the first time I came face to face with my own limitations. And so then another conclusion struck me: knowing myself had something important to do with the spiritual life.

So these two diametrically opposite experiences, one of God and one of failure, joined together, were the beginning of something for me. And yet I cannot tell you how to get these experiences. They are beyond our control. They come in God's good time. They cannot just be summoned up. Though I find it impossible to tell anyone how to achieve them, I know that their coming together is part of the spiritual life.

It is not our own doing

Shortly after those two experiences, reading what Christ had to say about not patching an old garment and about wineskins taught me an unexpected lesson. The spiritual life does not depend on my own efforts. It depends on God. What I have to do is 'put on the new garment', and leave the rest to the action of the Holy Spirit. I think this would be as good a place as any to begin.

It was about the time all these things were happening to me that I read through the whole of the New Testament. I was struck by many parts of it. One was the parable of the patch and the wineskins. I will take Matthew's version which is found in Mt 9:16-17.

The patches and the wineskins

'No one patches up an old coat with a piece of new cloth, for the new patch will shrink and make an even bigger hole in the coat. Nor does anyone pour new wine into old wineskins, for the skins will burst, the wine will pour out, and the skins will be ruined. Instead new wine is poured into new wineskins, and both will keep in good condition.'

There are two parables here. What the patches passage was saying to me was this: We spend a lot of time patching up our lives. We go on retreat, or we make a mission. We look into our lives and we see some of our faults. We say to ourselves, 'These are the things I must do something about. If only I could change these things my life would be better.' The list is more or less the same for all of us:

* There is some person I cannot get on with. Or perhaps I refuse to forgive.
* I am careless about my work and, as a result, others are suffering.
* I indulge in smoking or drinking or drugs, perhaps prescription drugs.
* I make no attempt to accept the inevitable crosses and sicknesses that come to me. Instead, I am angry, I rebel, I am jealous, I am moody.
* I am not giving enough time to prayer. Indeed, I may have given it up almost completely.

The list could go on and on. We say to ourselves, 'Now if only I could patch these things up, all would be well.' It is almost as if we pray, 'God, if you have any sense, these are the things you should fix up for me.' We proceed to patch up. We promise we are going to do something about these faults.

But next year, when I make my retreat again, I find the patch has fallen off. The tear is bigger. The fault is more deeply rooted. What is the solution? Christ does not give us a solution in this first parable. All he says is, 'No one patches up an old coat with a piece of new cloth.'

Perhaps the second parable will help us. It is about the wineskins.

The wineskins must be new
In Christ's time, though they had pottery, they continued to use wineskins. They stitched together the skins of animals, usually goats, and in some way made them leak-proof. The new skins were pliant and soft. When the new wine was poured into the skins it began to ferment. The skins were flexible and allowed the new wine to expand. But, apparently at times, perhaps to save money, people used old wineskins. However, they had become hard and tough and could not expand. So when the new wine fermented the skins burst. As Christ said, 'The wine will pour out and the skins will be ruined.' Besides, all the labour of

the wine-maker is lost. The conclusion is, new wine into new wineskins.

I applied this to to the first parable. Remember, Christ only said, 'Do not patch up an old garment.' He does not give us any positive advice. So perhaps what he is really saying is this, 'Do not bother patching the old garment. Rather, as with the wineskins, get a new garment. Throw away the old garment. Get a completely new one.'

A new garment

This made sense to me. When I continue patching up, when I say to God, 'Change this and that in me', I am really confining the action of God to my limited view of things. No doubt patching up will always be part of the process, because we must constantly keep trying to be better. But what God wants us to aim at is a new garment, a complete change in our lives. What we are hoping for in our lives is small and puny. God has greater things in store for us than we have ever dreamt of. 'What no one ever saw or heard, what no one ever thought could happen, is the very thing God prepared for those who love him' (1 Cor 2:9). In other words, what he has in store for us is beyond all imagining. It is a completely new garment.

What is this new garment? It is that marvellous, indefinable thing that Christ referred to in so many ways. It is the kingdom of God. It is the Holy Spirit. It is the pearl of great price. It is wisdom, enlightenment. It is transformation. It is the touch of God. It is this indescribable and precious thing that God wants to give us.

How does God go about giving us the new garment? It is a *process* that is going on all through our lives. I will try to describe the process.

CHAPTER 2

The process God uses to transform us

The story of the blind man Bartimaeus gives us an indication of how God goes about transforming us. You find it in Mark 10:46-52.

When Jesus and a large crowd were leaving Jerico, the blind beggar Bartimaeus was sitting by the wayside. When he heard that it was Jesus, he began to shout out in a loud voice, 'Jesus, son of David, take pity on me!' Did you notice the reaction of the people? They told him to keep quiet and even scolded him. They seemed to be saying, 'How could Jesus be interested in you? You are only a beggar and a blind beggar at that!' But he kept shouting all the more. Jesus stopped and called him. The attitude of the crowd changed immediately. They said, 'Cheer up. Get up. He is calling you.' He threw off his cloak, a valuable possession, and jumped up. You can almost see the crowd making a passage for him. He felt his way along until he reached Jesus. When Jesus asked what he wanted he said, 'Teacher, I want to see again.' Jesus said, 'Go, your faith has made you well' and at once he was able to see and he followed Jesus along the road. The prayer of the blind beggar could be ours. I like the older translation, 'Lord, that I may see.'

That is what Jesus wants to do for us, to help us to see. We often describe this as conversion, or to use the word I prefer, *transformation*. Among other things, Christianity is a religion of conversion, change, transformation. But how exactly does God go about changing us and transforming us?

The first stage: A deep dissatisfaction with our lives
I know most of us are frequently dissatisfied with our lives. We would all love to be more marvellous than we are. But that is not

the dissatisfaction I am referring to. It is rather a dissatisfaction
that is deeper and more persistent. I have often heard people describe it this way: 'Things in my life are going fairly well. My
work, my relationships, my interests. But somehow, I feel there
is something missing. I know there should be something more.
Perhaps my life is too comfortable. I have become too selfish. I
am too preoccupied with frivolous things. God seems to be ab-
sent.'

Or again, some ask, 'Was it for this I got married? Was it for this
that I am a Christian? Was it for this I was ordained? Was it for
this I became a religious? I keep on going and working, but I
have nothing to show for it. Surely there has got to be something
more and deeper in it.' These thoughts nag away at us.

My own dissatisfaction
The best example I can give is from my own life. In 1960 I was
appointed by my superiors in India as principal of a boys' high
school in Ambala, a military cantonment one hundred and
twenty miles north of Delhi. Most of the boys in the school were
army officers' sons. There were a few Catholics and Protestants
among them, but the majority were were Hindus and Sikhs. In
that part of the country, in those years, there was not a Muslim
in sight, otherwise we would have had them in the school too.
Gradually I began to ask myself, 'What have we got to offer
these non-Christians?' Indians have ancient religions and they
are a very spiritual people. In other words I was asking, 'What
exactly is Christianity? How does it differ from other great religions?' I had a Hindu teacher called Narindar who was a very
religious man. He used love to come to my office after school
and talk about religion. As with most Hindus, no matter what I
told him we Christians had, he said they had that too. We have
our Mass; they have their *puja*. We have prayer; they have that
too and, indeed, they may know more about it than many of us.
We have Christ; but all religions have their founders. The
Buddhists have Buddha, Muslims have Mohammed, the Sikhs
have Guru Nanak, Christians have Christ, another leader.

My Hindu friend really made me think and ask questions. I had never before been forced to think out my Christianity for myself. It was something I took for granted. The questions that kept coming up in my mind were these. 'What is the basic thing in Christianity? How does Christ differ from other religious founders? What have we Christians to give to the world?'

It was a difficult period for me. I know of others who left India because they could not solve this problem for themselves. However, it was a fruitful time and the search opened up so many other questions for me. Gradually, I got glimpses of an answer to some of the problems. After a lot of study and discussion and prayer, I realised eventually that what made Christ different from other religious founders was that he rose from the dead. For the first time I began to see the significance of the resurrection of Christ. The resurrection of Christ is the great message the Church has to give to the world. But that other question, 'What has Christianity to offer to the world?' started a deeper search in my life.

Now, for me, that was the dissatisfaction of which I am speaking here. I felt there was something missing in my life. I knew there had to be something more to Christ and Christianity. I knew the religious life must have a deeper meaning. And I was determined to find out what it was. It was only years later I saw that this dissatisfaction was indeed the beginning of conversion and transformation in my life. As a matter of fact, I am still searching, because conversion is constantly going on in us.

The second stage: A catalyst appears
Into this dissatisfaction something comes to act as a catalyst. A catalyst, a term from chemistry, is a substance which when put into other elements changes them completely. This catalyst, coming into our lives, changes us. It is God's way of speaking to us.

The catalyst is usually some event in our lives. It could be a very ordinary thing like making a retreat, reading a seminal book, meeting a person who turns out to be special, or simply a remark from someone. It could be a big event like a death, a change in work, a failure, an emotional upset, an illness. God communicates to each person in an individual way.

In every case, this catalyst, whatever it is, presents an alternative or the possibility of something greater. It brings a change of outlook. It is as if we say to ourselves, 'There is another way of looking at my problem. It is possible that things could be different.' A new hope begins to dawn. There is something to strive after. However, while all this is happening, we may not realise the significance of it all.

For me the catalyst was an Irish Christian Brother. While I was running that school in Ambala, the rest of the fathers in the community were constantly out giving missions and retreats in the north of India. I envied them, because I would have loved to see mysterious India. One of the fathers came back to tell me of an unusual brother he met in the Irish Christian Brothers' famous school in Bow Bazaar Street in Calcutta. My interest was aroused and I was anxious to meet him. Then, during the school holidays, I went to Calcutta to give a retreat and met the brother. In most ways he was an ordinary man. He had a great sense of humour. I imagine he was a good teacher from the way he communicated so much to me. But what was special about him was that when we met, he usually spoke of two things, God and prayer. He was certainly the catalyst for me because, after I listened to him things began to happen in my life.

The third stage: We begin to see things in a new way
Seeing things in a new way is one of the momentous elements in conversion. Indeed, it is like getting new sight. The prayer of Bartimaeus, 'Lord that I may see,' is answered for us. We begin to see so many things in a different way. The following are some of those things:

1. We begin to see God and Christ in a new way
I think this is one of the memorable things in any conversion. I have noticed that people who have gone through some kind of a

conversion talk about God in a way they could not have done before. Things which that brother in Calcutta said helped me to see God in a completely different way. He talked about God and Christ in the most intimate terms, as persons he really knew. He spoke of yearning to know them more deeply. As befitted the times, he used many scholastic terms. He spoke of the power, the beauty, the majesty of God, the infinity of God. He used to say to me, 'Think of the most beautiful person or the most magnificent scene you can imagine. God is a thousand times more beautiful. He is beyond anything we can imagine. He is a God who loves, who cares. He is not indifferent to me. He cannot be – he made me. There is a special bond between God and me.' I could have listened to the brother for ever and I can still remember many other things he said, so receptive was I. After I met him, the gospels and the psalms became alive for me. Indeed, the words seemed to jump off the page. I remember making remarks like this to some of my confrères: 'That gospel at Mass was full of meaning,' or, 'I never realised the psalms at Lauds were so full of praise.' The readings had never struck me so forcefully before.

That was the way I began to see God and Christ in a new way. Obviously for different people this stage develops in different ways. For some it goes on quietly deepening with nothing startling happening. For others it can come gradually to a climax. But this is only a beginning. *L 110, 261/ 248 / 4*

2. We begin to see prayer in a new way

In a conversion experience, besides seeing God in a new way, people usually begin to see prayer as something attractive. They speak about prayer in glowing terms. When people tell me that they are praying better, or are trying to pray better, I know that something has happened. What that brother said about prayer was again a catalyst for me. He spoke of advancing in prayer. He spoke of hours of prayer, of consciousness of God being present. He spoke of God coming in waves. He stressed yearning, even painful longing for God. Union with God was a phrase he often used.

All that was certainly new to me. Up until that I had thought of prayer as a futile struggle. I can recall the half hour of common meditation we had to make at six o'clock each morning and again in the evening. I was rarely able to get going. I spent most of the half hour day-dreaming and wondering would the time ever end. We never got off the morning meditation. So it was an enormous relief if the superior let us off the evening meditation and, better still, if he let us go to the pictures! And so, what the brother said about prayer was very different. It is true we had studied deeper prayer in Ascetical Theology, but it was as dry as dust and, besides, we were given to understand that all this was only for the exceptional few. And here was an ordinary man praying like that and talking of others who were praying the same way. I began to feel that deep prayer was possible. He opened up whole new avenues of prayer before me. I remember saying, 'I want to know God like that. I want to pray like that.'

A year or two later we closed the school in Ambala and I was changed to Bangalore. The great advantage in Bangalore was that we had a big seminary library there. I dug out books that were dusty from want of use and some of which were yellow with age. I devoured them. A big adventure began for me, which continues today in spite of my laziness and lapses and in-fidelity. I still read all I can on prayer and God. Of course my interest has broadened to scripture and theology and the religious life. But it was back in those early days that I discovered the classics of prayer: Poulain, Lehodie, Chapman and especially John of the Cross and Teresa of Avila.

3. We begin to see ourselves in a new way
This is the most painful part of transformation. We begin to see our real selves. That is one thing most of us are afraid of seeing. Then we stand face to face with ourselves perhaps for the first time in our lives. The sight is not too pleasant. Again, the way God goes about this is through some ordinary event in our lives. It could be an angry word from a companion, or a failure, an emotional upset, a death, a sickness. But in the event, whatever

it is, we see our faults and our weaknesses. At first we find it hard to accept. It can make us angry and rebellious. It has happened to me personally many times. I have often seen it happening to others. I have listened to others rebelling during retreats. Some weakness or fault to which they had paid little attention before, unexpectedly becomes clear to them. They cannot accept it. Their image of themselves is shattered. They become angry with themselves or with others. They even get angry with the director of the retreat. I have been the target a number of times! However, I can talk with understanding about the anger that wells up, because I went through it myself. I can remember every phase of the process, because I found it so painful.

I think this must have been the experience St Peter went through when he betrayed Christ and then 'broke down and cried' (Mk 14:66-72).

Though this stage is painful, it can be one of our most satisfying experiences when we come to terms with it.

The fourth stage: We begin to get a sense of purpose
When we are going through this process, it may take a long time to understand what has happened to us. I have been searching for ways of describing the outcome. Perhaps what Mark says in Mk 3:13-14, about the appointing of the apostles may describe it: 'Then Jesus went up a hill and called to himself the men he wanted. They came to him, and he chose twelve whom he named apostles. "I have chosen you to be with me," he told them, "I will also send you out to preach."'

This, indeed, has happened to us too. We have been called by Jesus, to be with Jesus and to go out to preach. When we realise this it gives us an awareness of a new purpose to life.

These, then, are the stages through which God usually leads us to transformation. At the time we do not know what is happening. Indeed, it may take years to discern the process. The start is usually dissatisfaction. Then there comes a catalyst, some person or event, which brings about a change in our outlook. It gives us new hope. Thirdly, we begin to see things in a new way. We look at God, and at prayer and at ourselves in a way we never did before. Fourthly, a sense of purpose comes into our lives. The dissatisfaction is replaced eventually by a sense of fulfillment

I will take up some of these elements and deal with them more fully.

PART II

We begin to see God in a new way

CHAPTER 3

Conversion transforms everything

A few years ago I was living in Clonard Monastery in Belfast. Towards the beginning of Lent I went into the refectory where a group of women, working in the house, were having a cup of tea. I joined them. They were discussing what they were giving up for Lent. They talked about giving up cigarettes or sweet things or drink. Some were doing something special like going to Mass or visiting a sick relation. I could not resist saying to them, 'So that is what Lent is? It is a time for giving up things or doing something hard?' They were indignant and said, 'Oh no, it depends on the motive.' We got on to discussing the possible motives. We could give up sweets to lose weight, or smoking or drinking because it is bad for the health, or drinking or gambling because it is expensive. We searched around for sometime, until one of the women said, 'We do hard things during Lent in order to come closer to God and to Christ.' That was as good a summing up of Lent as I have heard.

Conversion

Conversion is really what we were talking about. It came out in our discussion that there are two sides to conversion. I can be converted *from* something. I can be converted from sin or compulsions or bad habits, like excessive smoking or drinking. And that is a good thing. On the other hand, there can be a conversion *to*. I can be converted to something or someone, and that is the important thing. For the Christian the great thing is conversion to God and to Christ.

Of course, if there is conversion to God in our lives, the other things follow as the day follows night. We will try to give up sin and our bad habits. We will start going to Mass again. We will say our prayers. We will try to forgive. And so, conversion to God is what we should be seeking. Yet we seldom hear of this aspect of conversion, because most of our preaching has been about morals, about what we have to be converted *from*.

In the same way, we talk a lot about prayer and the church and the sacraments. And all these things are important. They are important because they bring God and the supernatural into our lives. But the important thing again is God and the supernatural.

God is the important thing

What is the supernatural? This may be a good way of describing it: This table I am working on is real. The furniture in the room, the house, the trees outside, the work we do, the relationships we have, these are all real. But there is another reality we cannot see or touch or feel. It is the world of the supernatural. It is the world of God the Father, the Holy Spirit and the Risen Christ. It is the world of the plan of God that St Paul often speaks of. This is another world and it, too, is real. It is the supernatural.

For some people this world of the supernatural seems unreal and far away. For others it is part of their lives. I doubt if we could be Christians without some sense of the Supernatural. Let me tell you a little incident.

One night, I was listening to a religious programme on the radio. There was sacred music and readings and a commentary. Among the readings was one from St Angela of Foglino which struck me very much. I do not remember the exact words nor have I been able to find them. It went somewhat like this: 'I look around and the world is full of God.' I think it is this realisation that transforms everything in our lives. When we realise that God is around us, we see everything in a different way:

* The universe becomes different. We look into the heavens and see the sun, the moon and the stars. Scientists talk of the big bang, of the expanding universe, of stars being born and stars dying, and of black holes. There is a constant evolution going

on in the vast universe. Is it this that St Paul speaks about in
Romans 8: 'The hope that creation itself would one day be set
free from its slavery to decay and would share the glorious
freedom of the children of God'? When I think of the mighty
universe I am aware that God is in this creation and in the
evolution that is going on. I am aware, too, that we are made
of the same stuff as the stars. The astronomers are really messengers explaining the mysteries of the universe to us. The
universe is God's and he is constantly working in it. Because
of that, it has to be respected.

* Nature, too, appears different. All around us in nature we see
constant birth and dying. In winter nature seems dead or
sleeping. But then in spring, the bare branches shoot forth the
buds. Then the leaves appear and after that the flower and the
fruit. We see lambs being born. Everything is coming back to
life. We can sense, perhaps, what Teilhard de Chardin called
'the within of things'. There is some force within pushing
things forward. Is this the Holy Spirit? God is in all nature.
Ecologists tell us of the delicate balance there is in nature. We
are in danger of destroying that balance by exploiting its resources. Ecologists, too, as God's messengers, remind us that
nature has to be respected.

* We see people in a different way. Shakespeare says in amaz-
ment, 'What a piece of work a man is.' Even the human body is
something wonderful. None of us could make a human eye.
There are faltering attempts to make a mechanical heart. And
yet nature produces these organs daily and with seeming ease.
But beyond that is the wonder and variety of the human spirit.
Men and women can soar to the heights and sink to the
depths. And so I have to respect the freedom and dignity of
every person, because God is the ground of their being. It is he
who keeps them in existence. With even more awareness now,
I can say with St Angela, 'I look around and the world is full of
God.'

What kind of a God?

But what kind of a person is this God? By reason alone we can come to the conclusion that God must be a being of power and might and majesty and intelligence. Only such a God could have made all these things. We can say little more than that because God is beyond our understanding. God is mystery.

However, there is a book that tells us a lot about this mysterious being. It is the Bible. The Jewish people had an experience of God and they wrote it down in the Old Testament. There God becomes alive for us. In the New Testament we have something even more intimate. It is Jesus' experience of God. He describes God as Father. He addresses him as Abba, an intimate name. Jesus tells us with absolute conviction that God is a Father who loves us and cares for us.

Do you remember where he said, 'For only a penny you can buy two sparrows.' In other words, sparrows are worth very little in our eyes. But Jesus goes on to say, 'Yet not one sparrow falls to the ground without your Father's consent' (Mt 10:29, 31). That is astonishing, because thousands of sparrows and millions of birds must fall to the ground in death every year. Some are devoured by predators, some are shot, some die of hunger or thrist, some are frozen. Yet, God knows when each one of those millions falls to the ground!

And then Jesus applies this to our lives. 'So do not be afraid; you are worth much more than many sparrows.' What he is saying is that God our Father knows each one of us intimately. Now if we know a few hundred people in a vague way that would be the limit. So what kind of a God is he who knows the millions of us in the world and knows everything about us? Not only does he know us, he cares for us, because we are worth much more than many sparrows. Yet, we find it so hard to believe that God is like that. We cannot see God as a Father who cares for us personally. An incident brought home to me how God cares for us.

God and us

About 1963, I was stationed in Bangalore in the south of India. In our community there was a young Redemptorist priest called Fidelis D'Sa. He was about to go to Louvain to study Church History. As he did not know French, a Belgian nun undertook to teach him. Since I was anxious to update my school-boy French, I asked if I could join their classes, if I were at home. They agreed. So I got to know the nun well. She was constantly telling me of a marvellous retreat that was preached to her sisters in Belgium by a theologian called Canon Guelluy, and she offered me a copy of it. I decided to use it for my own retreat for, at that time, we Redemptorists had to make our retreats on our own. So, when I started the retreat, I put the big bundle of sheets she gave me on the table in my room. I had a Bible on one side, since the retreat was based on scripture, and a French-English Dictionary on the other side. It was so badly typed and cyclostyled that I had to use a ruler to keep the lines straight. At first I had to look up many French words till I got used to his terminology. It turned out to be a marvellous retreat. I can still remember many things from it, but one sentence I have never forgotten. I can even remember the French. 'Dieu m'aime pour rien', 'God loves me for nothing.' In other words, God does not love me for what I did in the past. He does not love me because of what I will do in the future. He does not love me because I am better than others. He loves me for none of these things. He loves me *for nothing*. He loves me just because I am me. He loves me because he made me. He loves me because he still keeps me in existence. That was one of the most stunning things I had ever heard about God. He loves me personally and he loves me for nothing. Yet we find it so hard to believe that and do you know why?

Perfection

Many of us were brought up with the idea of *perfection*. Our aim as Christians was to seek perfection. Unfortunately, it was the wrong idea of perfection. When I was in the novitiate the theory was clear and simple: The better I become, the more God will love me. The fewer faults I have, the more God will favour me. So I determine that I am going to get rid of all my faults and become perfect. There was the classic way of doing that, called the Particular Examen. We took up one fault, we worked on it and examined ourselves on it every day until we overcame it. Then we moved on to another fault and overcame it too.

We Redemptorists had a similar technique in our Rule, called the Monthly Virtues. Each month had its virtue. January, February and March were devoted to faith, hope and charity, and so on with the other nine months. We examined ourselves on the virtue each day and there were books read on it at meals.

But I gave this up after some time. I have not that kind of mathematical mind. Besides, in the very unlikely event of overcoming all my faults, I would cease to be human! After all, having our weak side is part of the human condition. In any case, as St Paul discovered, we can never overcome all our faults, try as we will. Many of them just will not go.

What is perfection?
Perfection would seem to be accepting my faults and weaknesses and accepting that God accepts me with my weaknesses. Fr Van Breeman, in his excellent book, *As Bread that is Broken*, calls his first chapter, 'The acceptance of acceptance.' If only we could accept the fact that we are accepted by God. In a word, God loves us, faults and all. He loves us for nothing.

A free gift
So the love of God is not something we earn. It is not something he has to give us because we have done so many things for him. It is not a reward for a good life or for reaching perfection. The idea I used have was that if I were good enough, God would just have to notice me, like a teacher in class. Then one day he would come and give me the prize because I deserved it. Was I not better than others in the class? Then I would love him and my life of holiness would begin.

But then the despair came when I realised I could never get to the top of the class. I discovered my weaknesses would not go. I was always letting God down, or more truthfully, letting myself down.

That is not the way it works, thanks be to God. Otherwise I would never get there. God's love for us is a gift, a free gift. St Paul is constantly stressing this. He tells us we are not saved through our own works. It is not our own doing. It is God's gift. Our God is a God who constantly gives and gives gratituitously. God just gives and gives and for nothing, because that is the way God is. All we have to do is accept.

There is, of course, a human difficulty there. It is not easy to receive for nothing. Unless we were degraded by poverty, most of us would die of shame rather than hold out our hands begging, or go to the parish priest asking for a hand-out. We want to earn things and receive them as our due. We take pride in thinking, 'I got all I have by my own work.' It is humiliating to receive for nothing like a beggar. And so, perhaps without realising it, we say, 'No thank you God, not on those terms. I do not want your free gifts.'

On the other hand, when we come around to accepting that God loves us for nothing, when we are at ease with the gratuitousness of God's gift, then conversion to God has begun.

So God loves us for nothing. But because it is difficult to accept that, many ask me what all this is based on? What proof have I for presenting God in this way? Naturally, this is not my own idea. It is all found in the Bible. In the next chapter, I will present some of the passages that tell us most clearly that God loves me.

CHAPTER 4

God as seen in scripture

I was giving a mission in the huge parish of Donnycarney in Dublin. One morning I was out visiting the homes and came to a house and rang the door bell. There was a long delay and I was about to go when the door opened. Standing there was a young man of about twenty-five. From the way he looked at me, it was obvious he knew nothing about a mission in the parish and had not a clue as to who I was. So I told him I was one of the missioners. That meant nothing, so I added that there was a mission in the parish. He understood because he said, 'There is nobody in.' I said, 'But you are in.' He said, 'Oh, I am sorry, I mean my mother is not in.' Then he added, 'Would you like to come in?' I said, 'Yes.' So I told him about the mission and he said, 'But God wouldn't be interested in me.' I asked him why and he said, 'I have led a terrible life.' Before I knew he launched into his story. He had been brought up in the parish. He wasted his time at school and learned nothing. He left as soon as he could. He could not hold the few jobs he had. He got in with bad company and was soon drinking and gambling and womanising. He often went stealing. He decided to go to England and things got even worse there. He told me he was fortunate that he did not end up in jail. For a while he was on drugs. After years he came back to Ireland and now was, as he said, 'Sponging on my mother.' Then he said, 'Now do you see why God would not be interesed in me? I am not good enough. Your mission is meant for good people like my mother.'

I knew exactly what he was saying. I thought like that myself for years, and I imagine that many people think the same way. God is only interested in good people and I am not one. I wondered what I could say to convince him that God was interested in him. I tried to tell him that, with what success I do not know because I never met him again. But I thank him, because he put into words what I often thought. 'God is not interested in me. He is only interested in good people.'

If only we could accept that God loves us for nothing, how different our lives would be. But what is that based on? I know we can find parts of the Old and New Testament that emphasise the demanding God. There are passages like, 'It were better for him not to have been born.' Many of us were brought up with the 'God of the thunderbolt.' God is waiting to hurl it at us. But there are other passages that speak of God's love for us and I will concentrate on them. Here are a few of them:

The God of love in the bible
* I think some of the most beautiful expressions of God's love in the Old Testament are in Isaiah. Here is one: The Lord addresses Sion and also each one of us. 'Can a woman forget her own baby and not love the child she bore? Even if a mother should forget her child, I will never forget you. Jerusalem, I can never forget you! I have written your name on the palms of my hands' (Is 49:15-16).

The love of the mother for her child is the greatest human love there is. Mothers will usually do anything to protect their children. However, it can happen that a mother will hurt or injure her child. But God, never. He, or should we say She, will never forget us. Indeed, God the Mother has written our name in the palm of her hand.

* Isaiah 43:1-3: God is with us in our fears. 'Israel, the Lord who created you says, "Do not be afraid – I will save you. I have called you by your name – you are mine. When you pass through deep waters, I will be with you; your troubles will not overwhelm you. When you pass through fire you will not be burnt; the hard trials that come will not hurt you. For I am the Lord your God, the holy God of Israel who saves you."'

Fear is one of our most primitive emotions. But God who created us tells us there is no need to be afraid. He will save us and look after us in every danger whether it is water or fire or any other trial.

* Wisdom 11:23-12:1: This is another beautiful passage. 'For you love all things that exist, and detest none of the things that you have made, for you would not have made anything if you had hated it. How would anything have endured if you had not willed it? Or how would anything not called forth by you have been preserved. You spare all things, for they are yours, O Lord, you who love the living. For your immortal spirit is in all things.'

The fact that God created the universe means that God cannot be indifferent to us. It is not that he has created the universe and rolled it into space to look after itself, as if it were no longer God's concern. Far from it. God loves all of creation. God hates nothing in creation but is closely linked with it and with each one of us. God preserves us in existence. God's immortal spirit is in all things.

* God is love. 1 Jn 4:8-10: 'Whoever does not love does not know God, for God is love ... This is what love is: it is not that we have loved God, but that he loved us and sent his Son to be the means by which our sins are forgiven.'

Here St John does not merely say that God loves us. He says something more than that. He says, God *is* love. Love is God's very essence. If I could put it in more human language, without sounding blasphemous, God just has to love. That is the way God is! And notice what John says: it is not that I love him first and then he loves me in return, as a reward. No, he loves me first and then when I realise that, I love him in return.

In other words, we often think the order of events is this. For some reason or other, I begin to love God more and more and then God loves me in return. No, it is the other way about. God always loves me. Then one day I realise that and I love God in return. It is usually a feeling of absolute wonder when we do realise how much God loves us.

* Eph 2:8-9: 'For it is by God's grace that you have been saved by faith. It is not the result of your own efforts, but God's gift, so that no one can boast about it.'

This was the first text that brought home to me that we do not earn God's grace and love. It is not by our own efforts that we are saved and come to love God. No, it is a gratuitous gift, a gift that is given freely. So my former ideas of perfection were wrong. It is not that God will love us more, the more perfect we become. God knows we are not perfect and never will be. But that does not matter. God loves us as we are.

* *We flee from God*
Indeed, we are so reluctant to receive from God for nothing that we run away, we flee from God, because we feel we are not worthy, or that God would not be interested in me. This is the theme of Francis Thompson's great poem, 'The Hound of Heaven'. God is the Hound of Heaven, we are the prey. He seeks us, he pursues us. But we flee from him. The opening lines are well known.

I fled him, down the nights and down the days;
I fled him, down the arches of the years;
I fled him, down the labyrinthe ways
Of my own mind; and in the mist of tears
I hid from him.

When I look at my life, I find myself doing exactly that, running away from God. I am surprised at how I keep myself busy, doing unnecessary things. I find other things to do rather than write letters, or worse, rather than go to pray. All of us rush here and there, lest we stop and begin thinking. Perhaps we are trying to get away from God. It would be a good thing to ask ourselves from time to time, 'Is what I am about to do really necessary?'

* The Prodigal Son. Lk 15:11-32: This is Christ's strongest state-

ment of what he thought of his Father's love and forgiveness.
Unfortunately, the story has become stale for us, because we
have heard it so often. If only we could hear it as if for the first
time. Let us look at the story again from the place where the son
decides to return home. On the way home he prepares his confession, 'O Father, I have sinned before heaven and before you, I
am no longer worthy to be called your son.' The father sees him
in the distance and recognises him. Now, what would we have
done in that situation? Let's not give the answer we feel is expected of us. Let's be honest and realistic.

Let us suppose a son or a daughter of yours or a niece or nephew
ran away or left home against the wishes of the parents. Just to
vary the story let's take it as a 'she'. She has not communicated
with the family for years. Rumours have been coming back that
she has not been working and has been on drugs and drink and
even in jail. Her parents feel so ashamed. Then one day you are
in the house alone and the door bell rings. There is the girl standing at the door.

Now what would your reaction be? Remember, try to be honest
here! I could imagine a few possible reactions. You could say to
yourself, 'Look at that young hussy there. I wonder if she has
given one thought to all the suffering and shame and disgrace
she has brought to her parents and her family. I hope she will
have the grace to apologise and make up for it all.' And then you
bring her into the house with little enthusiasm. This would be a
woman's reaction, I imagine.

But there could be a *harsher* response, which would be more a
man's reaction. You could say, 'You are not coming in here! You
went off of your own free choice. You made your bed and now
you can lie on it. After all the agony you caused us, go and never
come back.' And then you close the door in her face. This was
the attitude of the elder brother. 'Him and his whores.' I think it
is realising our own anger that makes Christ's ending to the
story so unexpected. The father does not hesitate. He does not
say, 'Let the young blackguard come up to me and apologise.'

Without thinking, he runs down the road to greet the son. When the son starts his confession, the father is not interested in the details. He will get the details later. All that matters to him now is that his son has returned. He throws his arms around him and sends for the best robe.

Our 'mercy' is so different from that of the Father.

But who is the prodigal son?
We often think the prodigal son is the alcoholic or drop-out or the husband who has abandoned his wife or a prostitute. No, we are all the prodigal son. We have all fallen away from God in some way. For example, I do not murder, rob banks, commit adultery or hate. But I do know that the seed of every one of those is within me. I could murder or desire to possess things. I could commit adultery. I am a sexual being. I could hate. All of us could. Yet all these tendencies do not matter in the sight of God. They are part of the human condition.

When some people hear this way of looking at God they often say to me, 'Oh that is like Martin Luther's well known quotation, "Believe the more and sin the more."' (And by the way, Luther did not mean to go on sinning as much as you like!) What I am saying is this: Change will come about in my life the day I realise that God loves me and cares for me. The big stick or harshness never changed anyone. We have all heard the classic story of the orphan boy abandoned by his parents. He feels unloved. He rebels. The authorities may punish him and put him in jail. It will do no good. The only thing that will change him is love coming into his life. The day he falls in love with a woman and she with him, he changes. So with us. The day of our transformation is the day we have the realisation of being loved and wanted. Then we change and no one has to tell us to pray, to forgive, to act justly, to work for others. We just do it. And yet it so hard for us to believe this is how God will change us.

This is impossible

I was giving a retreat in Bombay in a convent which had been a Maharaja's Palace. There was a beautiful marble staircase leading from the entrance to the first floor, where the chapel was. I had to go up and down the staircase several times a day. One day I was coming down after speaking to the nuns. I had been talking about God's love for us, perhaps somewhat like I have written here. I heard footsteps coming down behind me as if someone were running after me. I did not look behind me, and just as I reached the ground floor a young nun caught up with me. She stood in front of me and said, 'But that is impossible.' I knew what she meant, but to get her story I asked, 'What is impossible?' She said, 'It is impossible that God could love me like that.' I asked why and she said, 'I am so bad.' I think that echoes the feelings of many of us. God could not be interested in me.

If only we could grasp this, that God loves me for nothing, everything in our lives would change immediately. If we are converted to God, then turning away from our sins and habits will follow. This could be the beginning of a complete transformation in our lives.

PART III

We begin to see Jesus in a new way

CHAPTER 5

Who is this man Jesus?

'But they were terribly afraid and said to one another, "Who is this man? Even the wind and the waves obey him!"' (Mt 4:41)

I think that every conversion, for a Christian, involves seeing Jesus in a new way. Certainly, that is what happened to me. Indeed I am surprised at how much my way of looking at Jesus has changed. We were not brought up on reading scripture. It may be hard to believe this but one of the most tedious subjects I had in the seminary was scripture. We had a text book, written in difficult Latin, and boring in the extreme. When we asked the professor a difficulty, he said, 'Now what does the author say?', and back to the boring old book we went!

Fortunately, some years later, in the 1960s, something exciting happened. Our Fr Sean Kelleher, a very good scripture scholar, returned to Bangalore from Rome. During the summer holidays he organised seminars on the Bible. I remember coming all the way from Ambala in the north of India to Bangalore in the south to attend. It was worth it because Sean brought us into a whole new world of scholarship. He made the Bible alive. Up until then, if scripture scholars proposed any new theory, they could be called to Rome and forbidden to teach or publish. This was the aftermath of the modernist heresy. But then in 1943 Pope Pius XII wrote a trail-blazing encyclical called *Divino Afflante Spiritu*, which encouraged scholars to study and present the latest biblical research. So Fr Sean brought the latest back from Rome. He told us about the form critics, demythologising, the new look at the infancy narratives, the kingdom, the resurrection and much more. It was all new and exciting. Suddenly reading the Bible became interesting. And, of course, we began to see Jesus in a new way.

The Jesus of my youth

Like most of my generation, I grew up with an uncomplicated idea of Jesus. It was easy enough to understand him. He was God. In some way or other, he was man, though that did not bother us too much. As befitting God, he was born in a miraculous way. He chose disciples and went about with them preaching and working startling miracles. He founded a church with his disciples. Then evil men conspired against him, though he was the best man who ever lived. They had him crucified. He died and rose again. Through his passion and death we were redeemed. However, the rising was important because it was another great miracle. It proved, beyond doubt, that he was God. His wonderful teaching was preserved in the New Testament. But the significant thing was that the church continued under the apostles and their successors, right up to the present day. The Roman Catholic Church was the true church. All we had to do was follow the teachings of Jesus and the church. If we went to Mass and the sacraments and said our prayers and kept out of sin, we, too, like the good thief, would go to heaven. It was a very cosy plan for living. We did not realise that it was not that simple.

However, when I was young, Jesus did not mean a great deal to us. Perhaps it was because on Sunday mornings we heard bits of the New Testament but did not really know it. As a result, when I became aware of God, I think I started off by being attracted to the Father. Indeed, most of the sermons and books we heard and read were about 'God' and little enough about Jesus, or Our Lord as we called him. Then when I started really reading the scriptures, it was an eye-opener to me. A different Jesus began to appear.

Who was the real Jesus?

Like Albert Schweitzer, I began 'The quest for the Historical Jesus'. I used to think, as did all of us, that Jesus was a man who brought a message from God. I gradually began to realise that he himself was important. Jesus himself was also the message.

What Schweitzer and others soon realised was that the gospels are not biographies or 'Lives of Jesus'. They are a picture of Jesus as seen by the early church. They were written years after Jesus died. Those who had lived with Jesus related stories about him and these were passed on by word of mouth, and eventually they were written down. There seem to have been two written sources for the gospels. The first is Mark's gospel itself, which was the first gospel to be written. The second source is what is called 'Q' which stands for the German word *Quelle*, meaning source. 'Q' is a collection of the sayings of Jesus. These sayings were incorporated in the gospels of Matthew and Luke. Now, while the gospels are not biographies of Jesus, we can learn a lot about Jesus from reading them.

A day in the life of Jesus
I read somewhere that the beginning of St Mark's gospel could be called, 'A day in the Life of Jesus'. To test this out once again, I have just stopped typing and reread the first three chapters of Mark. They are impressive. This is the kind of man I see emerging: Jesus suddenly appears on the scene. After his baptism, he came striding along the road with a message of hope. He was a man with good news, indeed, a man in a hurry. His message was clear and urgent. He told the people, 'The right time has come, and the kingdom of God is near. Turn away from your sins and believe the good news' (Mk 1:14).

And what an impact he made on those he met! He walked along the lake shore where he saw Peter and Andrew casting a net into the sea. He said, 'Follow me', and immediately they left their nets and followed him. A little farther on he met James and John and called them. They, too, followed him.

However, I think that John's version of the calling of Andrew gives us a different insight. (And it is difficult to reconcile it with the synoptic versions). Andrew and Peter and their group seem

to have been disciples of John the Baptist. They were obviously
awaiting the messiah with eagerness and were alert to any refer-
ence to him. So when Andrew heard John the Baptist say, 'Look,
there is the lamb of God', he wanted to find out more. Andrew
and his companion followed Jesus who invited them to come
and see where he lived. It was about four in the afternoon and
they spent the rest of the day with him. We are not told what
transpired at that meeting or what Jesus said. But the meeting
must have made a great impression on Andrew, judging by
what he did immediately afterwards. He searched for his brother
Peter and blurted out, 'We have found the Messiah.' So Peter,
with his usual enthusiasm, had to go to see this messiah of his
brother. Jesus at once marked Peter out as special. He changed his
name from Simon to Peter. He, too, was captivated immediately.

The next day Jesus decided to go to Galilee and there was another
memorable encounter. Jesus said to Philip, 'Come with me.'
Philip was so impressed that he met his friend Nathaniel and
told him that they had found the one Moses wrote about in the
book of the law. When Philip said he was Jesus from Nazareth,
Nathaniel could not resist asking, 'Can anything good come
from Nazareth?' I take it that was a kind of cant at the time, a
kind of 'Kerryman joke'. But then what Jesus said to Nathaniel
so swept him off his feet that he exclaimed, 'Teacher you are the
Son of God! You are the king of Israel!'

Crowds followed Jesus
It was the same everywhere Jesus went. He made an extraordinary impact on people. And this continued all through his short
public life. Crowds followed him. When people heard he was in
some place, there they gathered. At times, the house he was in
was so crowded that no one could get in. On one occasion, they
saw him travelling by boat and guessed where he was going and
ran around the shore to meet him when he arrived. I have no
doubt but that, on the way, they called others and the crowd
grew. On another occasion, thousands followed him for more
than a day, even though they had nothing to eat. Matthew puts

the number at 5,000 men, not counting women and children. Very often Jesus was so mobbed and lionised that he and his disciples had not even time to have a meal. Indeed, this got so bad that at times he would not go into the towns but stayed in country places to avoid the crowds. All this was particularly so when he was in Galilee, but even when he started his journey to Jerusalem, and opposition was growing, he still attracted crowds.

Why did *Jesus attract people?*
It is very hard to put into words what attracts one person to another. It must have been his magnetic personality. However, apart from his personality there were two other reasons. His preaching and his miracles. I suppose the two happened together. Yet Luke implies his preaching was the first thing to attract notice. He introduces Jesus's public life in this way: 'He began to teach in their synagogues and was praised by everyone' (Lk 4:15). On the other hand, Matthew and Mark say the preaching and the miracles came together.

His preaching
If preachers were anything like they are today, the usual rabbis must have been an uninspiring lot! Perhaps many people slept through the sermons they heard. And then Jesus appeared on the scene. Mark says, 'They were astounded at his teaching.' They asked, 'Is it some kind of new teaching?' He taught like one having authority, and not as the scribes. He said to them, 'You have heard it was said to those of ancient times ... but I say to you ...' He spoke of God in a new way. He presented God as a loving Father who cares for his children. Jesus himself felt great compassion for the people and told them there was no need to worry. His message was, above all, a message of hope. He constantly reminded them that the kingdom of God was at hand. He told memorable stories and used graphic imagery from everyday life, as we can see from his parables. They listened, enthralled.

When it came to human relations, what he had to say was new.

He told the people to love one another and above all to forgive. No longer was it 'an eye for an eye and a tooth for a tooth', but 'I say to you ... if anyone strikes you on the right cheek, turn the other also' (Mt 5:38-39).

He taught them how to pray. He urged them to seek the will of his Father, just as he himself did.

His miracles

His first miracles, too, must have taken all by surprise. They were unexpected and he worked them from the beginning of his preaching. Matthew says he went 'all over Galilee, teaching in the synogogues, preaching the good news about the kingdom and healing people who had all kinds of disease and sickness. The news about him spread through the whole country of Syria' (Mt 4:23-24). And Matthew goes on to say, 'Great crowds followed him from Galilee, the Decapolis, Jerusalem, Judea, and from beyong the Jordan' (Mt 4:25).

The people came asking for miracles, sometimes in crowds, at other times singly. 'That evening, at sundown, they brought to him all who were sick or possessed with demons. And the whole city was gathered around the door' (Mk 1:32-33). Or it was the leper or a blind man who came alone asking for a cure.

Of course, everywhere he went he met people who were suffering and in need. Then those who were healed, or those who saw the miracles, told others. The news of his miraculous powers spread like wildfire and crowds came. This is easy for us to understand, because it is no different today. If a rumour of miracles at some place gets around, crowds will gather. If someone gets a reputation for the gift of healing, people flock around him or her. The newspapers and television will be full of it. I am sure it was even more so in the time of Christ when medicine was very primitive. You can imagine the impact of all this when he first appeared. And this, of course, was only the beginning. There was more to come, both wonderful and terrible.

And yet this was a different Jesus

All I have just said about his preaching and his miracles, I would have accepted when I was young. But then I began to notice that, in ways, this was a different Jesus from what I had imagined. Take for example the miracles I have just been talking about. No doubt his miracles were impressive, but Jesus did not want to spend his whole life working wonders. He had other important work to do. This came across to me from the story in Mark 1:29 and following. Jesus and his disciples left the synagogue and went to Peter's house, where he cured Peter's mother-in-law. That evening the people brought all who were sick to the front door of the house and Jesus healed them. But then, Mark continues: 'Very early the next morning, long before daylight, Jesus got up and left the house. He went out of the town to a lonely place, where he prayed. But Simon and his companions went out searching for him, and when they found him they said, "Everyone is looking for you."

But Jesus answered, "We must go to the other villages round here. I have to preach in them also, because that is why I came." So he travelled all over Galilee, preaching in the synagogues and driving out demons' (Mk 1:35-39).

What that passage says to me is this: Jesus realised that when the people eventually heard of his miraculous powers, they would keep coming. He knew his whole life could be swallowed up in working miracles. Indeed, he could have been occupied in that one place for a long time. Though the miracles and driving out demons were part of his mission, he also had to preach the word to other people. He had to keep moving, and that is what he did. 'So he travelled all over Galilee, preaching in the synagogues and driving out demons.'

So his preaching and his miracles were factors in spreading his fame and attracting people to him.

But was he gentle Jesus meek and mild?

Apart from his own attitude to miracles, I began to notice other things I had not averted to before. We used recite the verse 'Gentle Jesus meek and mild'. But was that the real Jesus? Was he the kind of Sacred Heart image some people still have? The gospels make it clear he was anything but! There was a toughness in him. He could stand up to anyone. He had hidden depths that appeared only gradually. I began to see a different, more powerful Jesus, and he intrigued me. Indeed, he baffled the disciples too. They could not make him out. At times, they were not only overawed, but even afraid of him. In the story of the storm at sea we can see that.

Who is this man?

Jesus was crossing the lake in a boat with the disciples. He must have been exhausted because he fell asleep. One of those sudden storms that are common in the lake of Galilee, blew up. The boat was probably a frail craft and it began to fill with water. Understandably, the disciples were terrified and thought they were about to die. Though they woke Jesus and asked for his help, they were overawed at the outcome. I am still surprised at how Mark finishes the story: 'But they were terribly afraid and said to one another, "Who is this man? Even the wind and the waves obey him!"' (Mk 4:41).

I get the feeling that even when they got to know Jesus better and became more attached to him, the awe never quite left them. They probably continued to ask, 'What kind of a man is he?' Indeed, they gradually saw many different sides to his character. For example, they were probably worried when they heard him dispute with the Scribes and Pharisees. There were no punches pulled in these encounters.

His struggle with the Pharisees begins

Gradually we begin to see in the gospels the antagonism between Jesus and the Scribes and the Pharises. Obviously there was a fundamental difference between them. One issue they clashed on was the basis of the authority of each. For the Scribes and Pharisees, their authority rested on the law of Moses. And down the centuries, they interpreted it in their own way. Eventually they ended up with 613 regulations, which each good Jew was expected to follow. Of course, it was impossible for anyone to follow all of them to the letter. Now, Jesus did not question the law of Moses. Indeed, he had come to fulfil the law and the prophets. But he did question their interpretation of it.

Take the laws of ritual washing: It was even laid down how much of the arm one had to wash and how vessels should be purified. These were purely ritual washings, not for hygienic purposes. The devout Jews observed them scrupulously. However, Jesus considered them relatively trivial. Or take the laws connected with the sabbath: These were the strictest of all the laws, yet he considered himself Lord of the Sabbath. Again, Jesus presented his six well-known antitheses in Matthew 5:21-48. An antithesis is a stating of contrasting ideas. Jesus presents the old version of the law and then his own interpretation – 'You hear that it was said ... but now I tell you.' He was his own authority. Indeed, Jesus put the personal needs of the people before conventional rules. He even cured the sick on the sabbath. All this must have been galling to the Scribes and the Pharisees, for they thought that their personal salvation depended on the exact observance of these laws. But his strongest words are in Matthew 23 and in Luke 11. These chapters are a merciless diatribe on their hypocrisy. He says a number of times, 'How terrible for you Pharisees.' He tells them. 'You put loads on peoples' backs which are hard to carry, but you yourselves will not stretch out a finger to help them carry those loads' (Lk 11:46). We know that they were seething with anger after this attack. St Luke continues, 'The Pharisees began to criticise him bitterly, trying to lay traps for him and catch him saying something wrong' (Lk 11:53).

Jesus continued to denounce them because they were not helping their people to be true Israelites.

Jesus' attitude to certain classes of people
This was another bone of contention. The Scribes and Pharisees constantly objected to the so-called doubtful company he kept. He was constantly in the company of tax collectors and sinners.

What was even more scandalous, he ate meals with them and invited himself to their dinners. With them he carried on his well known 'table-fellowship', a special sign of accepting someone. He allowed women of doubtful morals to touch him. He associated with Samaritans, the traditional enemies of the Jews, and made one of them the hero of one of his stories. He worked miracles for gentiles. In a word, he overrode the conventions and taboos of the legalistic Jews. He did this to show that he welcomed every man and woman, even those who were not ritually clean. To him all men and women were equal and all were loved by his Father. His answer to those who objected was, 'People who are well do not need a doctor, but only those who are sick. I have not come to call respectable people, but outcasts' (Mk 2:17).

So for Jesus the law should be interpreted by the dual commandment of love of God and love of one's neighbour. However, he did not want this love to descend into sentimentality. It was to be unselfish service of others until it hurt. To love God and to love one's neighbour was the guideline.

As we read the gospels, we can see how the antagonism grew after each encounter. The chief priests and the elders were so angry that they 'made plans to arrest Jesus secretly and put him to death' (Mt 26:4). They felt they had to get rid of him.

The Jews today

Living here in Belfast in these days of ecumenism, many of us have become sensitive to the reactions not only of Protestants but also of Jews. I am aware of how hurt the Jewish people are by the seeming anti-Jewish tone of parts of the New Testament. Jesus did have a running battle with some of his fellow Jews, especially the Pharisees. Now, the Pharisees were committed people and wanted to protect the law. But Jesus did not approve of their interpretation. This has been described as 'in house' quarrelling, Jew disagreeing with Jew. Indeed, the new Jesus movement was looked on as a kind of sect of Judaism. Jesus and his followers prayed and worshipped in the temple. However, after the Resurrection attitudes began to change. The Christian claim that Jesus was the long awaited Messiah was emphasised. This led to a growing split between the synagogue and the Christians. Then after 70AD the Christians were expelled from the synagogue. As after any split, the usual suspicions and vituperations began. They increased as the years went by.

It was at this time that the gospels were written. So what the evangelists wrote reflected the opposition between the Christians and the Jews after 70AD. Forty years after Jesus died, they read back into the ministry of Jesus, issues which applied to their own time. Indeed, in St John's gospel, which was written later than the other three, the antagonism is even stronger. So it is this post-70 view of the Jews we Christians are presented with when reading the New Testament today.

Now this does not answer the whole problem. Nor does it excuse the anti-semitism that increased down the centuries and the dreadful persecution and pograms that followed. But we are aware of the hurt and pain of the Jews to whom we owe so much.

He challenged his disciples

But this disconcerting Jesus did not make things easy for his disciples. He gradually began to talk to them about his own future suffering and death. He went on to tell them that they too would suffer. He asked sacrifices of them. Indeed, some left him because what he said was a hard saying. He went so far as to tell them that he came to cast fire on the earth and he would that it be kindled. He even admitted his teaching would set mother against daughter and son against father (Mt 10:34-36). He implied they might have to lay down their lives.

So his message was a mixture of joy and hope on the one hand and challenging demands on the other. Those who heard him were either against him or for him. They wanted to put him to death or they wanted to be his disciples. They could not be indifferent. Naturally opposition began to grow, even in Galilee.

His journey to Jerusalem

Eventually I discovered, from studying the gospels, that the writers had a definite plan. The outline of his public ministry is a journey to Jerusalem. He started in Gallilee. (John has Jesus starting first at the festival in Jerusalem and then going to Galilee because his life was threatened. It is difficult to reconcile these two versions. I will stay with the synoptics.)

In Galilee at the beginning he went to the synagogues on the sabbath. He was well received, but then he began to anger the authorities. Their support waned. Crowds of ordinary people still came but he spoke to them in the open or at the seashore. He did a lot of his preaching in private with his disciples. It was probably then that he revealed to them 'the secrets of the king-dom of God'.

Jesus sensed the growing opposition and began to reveal to his disciples that he would go to Jerusalem and be rejected, mocked, made to suffer and be done to death. But then he would rise again on the third day. The disciples did not want to hear this. Indeed, Peter called Jesus aside to remonstrate that a messiah could not be rejected and done to death. The disciples wanted a victorious messiah. But Jesus said, 'Get behind me Satan.' He refused to be tempted by this soft option. Twice more he an-nounced his future suffering and death. He continued his jour-ney from Galilee along the border of Samaria to Jerusalem. The disciples thought that his triumph would come when they reached the city. Luke tells us, 'He was now almost at Jerusalem, and they supposed that the kingdom of God was just about to appear' (Lk 19:11). Things did seem to be going that way. On Palm Sunday, Jesus did make a triumphant entry into Jerusalem.

But the triumph did not last long. St Luke tells us what hap-pened on the days following Palm Sunday: 'Every day Jesus taught in the temple. The chief priests, and the teachers of the Law, and the leaders of the people wanted to kill him, but they could not find a way to do it, because all the people kept listening

to him, not wanting to miss a word' (Lk 19:47-48). Eventually, on
Holy Thursday, they arrested him in the Garden of Olives. They
decided this was the time to kill him.

Why was he killed?
The reason is not clear. Before the Sanhedrin, the only accusa-
tion they agreed on was that he blasphemed. Before Pilate, he
was accused of claiming to be Son of God and to be king. But
more explicit charges of capital offences against the Roman State
are recorded by Luke. He tells us that the whole council of the
Jews brought Jesus to Pilate and began to accuse him. They said,
'We caught this man misleading our people, telling them not to
pay taxes to the Emperor and claiming that he himself is the
Messiah, a king. ... With his teaching he is starting a riot among
the people all through Judaea. He began in Galilee and now has
come here.' (Lk 23:2, 5) Was the council presenting a political
charge of rioting or a charge of blasphemy?

In the eyes of the Romans this was really a charge of sedition,
which is incitment to public disorder. The Romans in the
provinces used crucifixion as a deterrent against sedition. Are
we, then, to conclude that Jesus was crucified under Pontius
Pilate for sedition?

That goes against the facts of Jesus' life and, indeed, he denied it
himself. Besides, if he had been seditious, why were his followers not arrested, as they would surely be involved? And we
know they were not prevented from preaching after his death.
So sedition could not have been the real reason.

Then we could ask, what made the Sanhedrin present these
accusations? I suppose there were many reasons, because they
had so many things against him. For example, Jesus' refusal to
accept their interpretation of the law; his flaunting legal and social
taboos; the strong language he used in Mt 23 and Lk 11 which
would have lowered their authority in the eyes of the people; he
exposed their vested interest in making money by selling and
exchanging in the temple. As Mark said of Pilate, 'He knew very

well that the chief priests had handed Jesus over to him because they were jealous' (Mk 15:10).

Though he found no cause against him, Pilate, after a struggle to save Jesus, condemned him to be crucified because he was afraid of being denounced to Caesar.

And so it was that Jesus died a painful, humiliating death. This must have been a terrible blow to the disciples. After two glorious years, their dreams were shattered. There was no kingdom. Instead Christ died as a criminal. He was a failure. This seemed to be the end of the great adventure. Some started drifting back to their boats and their former lives.

Then his triumph

But then on Sunday morning a rumour started to do the rounds. 'Did you hear the latest? The Lord has arisen and appeared to Simon.' The disciples did not expect this and at first many of them refused to believe. It annoys me to see that they paid no attention to the reports of the women. But Jesus appeared to different people and to different groups. Gradually they accepted the resurrection of Jesus, and now they had something to tell the world.

It was indeed a startling message. There was a man called Jesus, who lived and died but then he arose again. And that Risen Christ was alive and with them. This was a message worth telling to others. A message worth laying down one's life for.

And my image of Jesus was certainly changing.

CHAPTER 6

The Resurrection

When we started studying scripture again in the 1960s, the most thrilling thing we heard was the new interpretation of the resurrection. A book, called *The Resurrection*, had just appeared some years earlier. It was by Fr Francis Xavier Durrwell, a French Redemptorist. It is one of those great seminal books and made an important impact on the generation of theologians immediately before Vatican II. What a contrast it was to the old theology! I, for one, was really excited about it, as it helped me to see Jesus in a new way.

The old theology of the resurrection
Before Vatican II we were told that the important thing in the life of Christ was that he died to redeem us. Mankind had sinned and was separated from God. God in his love decided to save the human race. His own Son, Jesus Christ, came on earth as a man. He was sinless. To make reparation for our sins, he died in obedience to the will of his Father. By this act of obedience he made satisfaction for our sins. He redeemed us or bought us back from the power of Satan. The price had been paid. Then three days later he arose. The resurrection was God's reward to his Son, and it was an apologetic proof that Jesus was God.

The new theory of the resurrection
Durrwell does not agree that the resurrection was, as he puts it, an epilogue or an appendix to the story of redemption. He insists that the drama was not brought to a close at the ninth hour on Good Friday, with Easter merely telling us what happened to the hero.

Rather, Durrwell maintains that scripture sees it differently.

According to the New Testament, the resurrection was as much a part of the redemption as his death. This he sets out to prove.

1. The synoptics begin with Jesus announcing the approaching kingdom. But then a new element comes into the story. Jesus begins to tell his disciples that he would go to Jerusalem and be killed and on the third day be raised from the dead. The dying and the resurrection are really one act. As St Luke says, in the Road to Emmaus story, 'Was it not necessary for the Messiah to suffer these things and then to enter his glory?' (Lk 24:26). His death was the first act and the second his resurrection. It was in this way he entered his glory.

2. St John, too, takes up this idea of glory. Indeed, two of his great themes are 'His hour' and his 'glorification'. Jesus was aware of this towards the end of his life and especially at the last supper. St John says, 'It was now the day before the Passover Festival. Jesus knew that the hour had come for him to leave this world and go back to the Father' (Jn 13:1) Then later on, towards the end of the last supper, Jesus prays, 'Father the hour has come. Give glory to your Son, so that the Son may give glory to you' (Jn 17:1-5). His glory was to be his dying and his rising again. Jesus knew that he was about to die and rise again. It was in this that his Father would glorify him.

This glorification did, in fact, take place when Jesus has passed through the 'hour' of his death and resurrection to the Father in glory.

3. St Paul sees both the death and the resurrection of Jesus as necessary for redemption. Indeed, he constantly contrasts the two. Jesus had to die and Jesus had to rise. 'Because of our sins he was handed over to die, and he was raised to life in order to put us right with God' (Rom 4:25).

In our baptism, St Paul sees us dying with him and rising with him. 'By our baptism, then, we were buried with him and shared his death, in order that, just as Christ was raised from death by the glorious power of the Father, so also we might live a new life. For since we have become one with him in dying as he did,

in the same way we shall be one with him by being raised to life
as he was' (Rom 6:4-5).

This way of looking at the resurrection, as presented by
Durrwell, is generally accepted today. For the first time we
heard the expression, 'the Paschal Mystery'. Easter is, of course,
the important feast of the church year. And the conclusions that
flow from it are surprising.

Jesus was a man

This was one of the first things I had to learn. The full implica-
tions of this theory make sense only if we keep in mind that
Jesus was a man. A little incident brought this out for me.

A traditional Catholic's view of Jesus

I remember years ago I was giving a mission in Bombay. One
Sunday morning I was out visiting families and I came to a big
block of flats. When I reached the top landing there were two
doors. I knocked at one but there was no reply. I did notice that
the name was Catholic. When I rapped the second door it was
opened immediately. There was a lovely Catholic couple with
their teenage children waiting for me. Indeed, they had a son in
Goregaon, the local seminary. Yes, of course, they would certainly
come to the mission, both morning and evening. Just before I left
I said, 'I see the people across the landing are Catholics. They
might wonder why I did not call, so would you please tell them I
invite them to the mission?' There was dead silence! No one ut-
tered a word until the lady of the house said, 'We cannot do that,
we are not talking to them.'

A few days later I met the lady again and she told me the story.
In Bombay, people who made some money in places like the
Persian Gulf, often invested it in building a block of flats. It
meant they had their own appartment to live in and got rent
from the other apartments. So she was the landlady. The family
across the landing were the tenants. There was the usual friction.
She told me they were misusing the flat. They pulled switches
and taps off the wall. They did not keep the flat clean. They

threw refuse out the window. But worst of all, they insulted her family. I suggested they try to make it up during the mission. She said, 'Do you expect us to forgive them after the way they treated us?' In an attempt to say something to convice her I suggested, 'But look at Christ. He was a good man and he was treated badly. Yet he forgave his persecutors.' Her answer was, 'It was easy for Christ. He was God.'

Jesus was one of us

The lady's answer astonished me. I asked myself, 'Is that the way we think about Jesus?' In a way I suppose it was, though we would not put it so bluntly. That was a very Catholic idea, that Jesus after all was God. Of course it was obvious at once that it did not make sense. If it was easy for Jesus that meant he did not really suffer. And if he did not really suffer, then his passion and death were a big comedy. He was just play-acting, pretending to be a man. And the whole gospel story was a big farce. For the gospel to ring true, Jesus had really to suffer. That meant he had to be a man.

That was the theology of the Church from the beginning. It was the doctrine of the incarnation. Christ was both God and man. It meant that, while Jesus was God, he was man too. He was as fully human as you or me or any man or woman.

That is what the resurrection is about. It is about a man. It is about a man who was God. But it is about a man. It is about one of us, a human being. That makes all the difference in understanding Jesus who was raised from the dead.

The effects of the resurrection

The resurrection of this man Jesus was not a mere resuscitation, a mere revival or return to life. It was not Jesus in the same body, brought back again. No, it was a glorification. The humanity of Jesus was brought into the Divine. Jesus, the Word, had returned to the Father. His body was now a glorified body. St Paul tells us what this meant: 'For we know that Christ has been raised from death and will never die again – death will no longer rule over him. And so because he died, sin has no power over him; and now he lives his life in fellowship with God' (Rom 6:9-10).

His glorification also meant something more. The New Testament books begin to give Jesus a new title. He is Lord. Jesus had now become Lord of all. The kingdom was approaching closer. Eventually all things will be placed under his rule. As Jesus said before his ascension, 'All power is given to me in heaven and on earth' (Mt 28:18).

Something new happened to Jesus the man
Jesus Christ was a man. Like any man or woman he suffered. He suffered hunger and thirst. He was hounded by the Scribes and the Pharisees who hated him because of their jealousy. He suffered physical pain and mental anguish. He died a long, lingering, painful death. He suffered the anguish of thinking his Father had abandoned him. But now all that is past.

Something extraordinary has happened to him. St Paul says, 'Christ will never die again – death will no longer rule over him … sin has no power over him' (Rom 6:9-10).

That means he has conquered death. He has conquered sin and all its effects. He is the victor over sin and death. The consequences of sin can no longer touch him. He will no longer suffer hunger or thirst. He will never again be subjected to hatred and jealousy. He will never suffer pain or any of the ills and weaknesses of men and women. He is beyond it all. He is with the Father. He is glorified.

Something new happened to us
But Jesus did not die and rise for himself alone. Just as Adam's sin effected all of us, so the death and resurrection of Jesus is for all us. His victory is our victory too. His resurrection is our resurrection too. St Paul insists on this: 'For just as all people die because of their union with Adam, in the same way all will be raised to life because of their union with Christ' (1 Cor 15:22).

So, because of the resurrection, all men and women are changed. The Holy Spirit has been release in us. One day, like Jesus, we will die. But he has gone before us, the first fruits of the resurrection. We too will rise again. And we, too, will be the victors over sin and death. We will never again suffer hunger or thirst, or pain or hatred or jealousy. We, too, will go to the Father. We will share the glory of Jesus the man. It will be a new kind of existence. St Paul puts it this way: 'What we suffer at this present time cannot be compared at all with the glory that is going to be revealed to us' (Rom 8:18).

In the meantime we have a great reassurance. The Risen Christ is with us here and now. Just as God our Father is always present, so too is the Risen Christ. And then, he is going to come again. At the end of time he will come in glory. We are reminded of this in the new liturgy after Vatican II. After the consecration we have that glorious proclamation of faith, 'Christ has died. Christ has Risen. Christ will come again.' In the early church they were so aware of this that they thought Christ would come again in their own life time. Gradually they realised that his second coming, the *parousia*, was not going to happen for a long time. We are still waiting. But we have this assurance that the Risen Christ is with us and that he will come again at the end of time.

In this way, my search for the real Jesus went on for a long time. I became more and more intrigued with what I learned of him. The cosy Jesus of my youth no longer satisfied me. Yet I knew I had not fathomed the mystery of Jesus. There was so much more to learn, more than I will ever grasp.

CHAPTER 7

Faith in Jesus and in God

Years ago in India I made a memorable journey. If you know a little of the geography of the country you may be able to follow the route I travelled. I left Bangalore one morning and after a day and a night in the train I arrived the next morning in Bombay. I went to our house in Chembur and spent the night there. Early the next morning I went to the docks and boarded a ship for Karachi in West Pakistan. It was a beautiful calm journey of twenty-four hours, and the following morning I arrived in Karachi. We preached missions for about six weeks there. Then Fr Gerry Morgan and I went by train to Lahore where we preached a school retreat to girls. We then crossed the border back into India and for the first time I saw Amritsar, the home of the Sikhs, away in the north of India. Then on to Ambala and Delhi where I took a train for Madras which is in the south, on the east coast. That was a journey of about two days and a night in the train. From Madras I went right across the country to Kerala which is on the west coast. After some retreats there I went back to Bangalore. Altogether the journey took a couple of months and I covered a good part of India. It was a mighty treck and the best geography lesson I ever had. Covering so much ground at one go was memorable. But for me there was something even more memorable. That was also a journey into Jesus.

A journey into the New Testament
During that journey, on the train, on the boat, in the places where I stayed and worked, I read the whole of the New Testament. Often, before that, I had had a yearning to know more and more about Jesus. In that reading, the message of Jesus

came across to me in a way I had never anticipated. I saw many things in a completely different way. I was really shaken and disturbed and yet gladened by what I read. To this day I remember some of the insights that struck me in the gospels. I found startling things in the letters of St Paul, which I marked. I took notes of gospel passages at the back of the book. I have just been looking them up, because I still have the actual book I used. It is the translation by Ronald Knox that my sister gave me when I was leaving for India. And so I look back on those couple of months not only as a journey across India, but even more as a journey into Jesus. It was then that the New Testament began to mean something to me. But even more so, it was the time Jesus began to become alive to me.

Many passages in the New Testament excited me, but I have already spoken of the one that impressed me most. It was Ephesians 2:8-9. This is Knox's version: 'Yes, it was grace that saved you, with faith for its instrument; it did not come from yourselves, it was God's gift, not from any action of yours, or there would be room for pride.'

I read and re-read the passage. It came as a surprise to me that being saved does not come from any action of my own. I thought I had to strive manfully to save my soul. It was I, myself, who had to do it. But no, St Paul told me that being saved is a gift of God. And God's instrument is faith. So then, if I believe in Jesus, I am saved.

For me these were two completely new ideas. First, we are not saved by doing things. We used think it depended on the number of prayers we said or the amount of penance or the frequency of the sacraments or devotion at Mass. These are very helpful. But they alone do not save us. Secondly, we are saved through faith. But what exactly does that mean?

What is faith?
Up until that time, I thought faith was a mental decision. In theology we learned that faith was an intellectual assent to the

teachings of the church. Great emphasis was put on accepting the list of the fundamental truths of the church. For example, we renewed our faith at Sunday mass by saying, 'I believe in God the Father almighty … I believe in the Holy Ghost … I believe in the resurrection of the dead … etc.' Again we went through that list when we renewed our vows at Easter and at missions.

Or I used think that having faith was the opposite of being an atheist. The atheist did not believe in the existence of God, while I believed that he did exist. So I had faith. And I suppose that is one way of looking at faith.

But then, from reading the gospels, faith seemed to be something different. Obviously, that was not what Jesus meant when he spoke of having faith and he spoke about that often. He did not say to the people, 'Do you believe this or that doctrine of the Church?' So I searched through the gospels for the places where Jesus demanded faith.

What did Jesus mean by faith?
Every time Jesus worked a miracle, there was just one thing he demanded and that was faith. The cure of the two blind men, in Mt 9:27-31, is a good example: 'Jesus left that place, and as he walked along, two blind men started following him. "Take pity on us, Son of David!" they shouted. When Jesus had gone indoors, the two blind men came to him and he asked them, "Do you believe that I can heal you?" "Yes, sir!" they answered. Then Jesus touched their eyes and said, "Let it happen then just as you believe!" – and their sight was restored.'

The one thing Jesus wanted to know was this, "Do you believe I can heal you?" Jesus seemed to be saying, "Do you believe I have the power? Do you trust me?" Believing here means having trust and confidence in Jesus.

However, faith is not only knowing that Jesus has the power, but also being convinced that he wants to help others. In Mt 8:1-3 we have this little story: 'Then a man suffering from a dreaded skin-disease came to him, knelt down before him and said, "Sir, if you want to, you can make me clean." Jesus stretched out his hand and touched him. "I do want to," he answered. "Be clean." At once the man was healed of his disease.'

So by faith we also believe that Jesus wants to help us.

The paralysed man

There is another good example of faith in the story of the para-lytic being lowered through the roof. It is in Mk 2:1-5: 'A few days later Jesus went back to Capernaum, and the news spread that he was at home. So many people came together that there was no room left, not even in front of the door. Jesus was preach-ing the message to them when four men arrived, carrying a paralysed man to Jesus. Because of the crowd, however, they could not get the man to him. So they made a hole in the roof right above the place where Jesus was. When they had made an opening, they let the man down, lying on a mat. Seeing how much faith they had, Jesus said to the paralysed man, "My son, your sins are forgiven."'

I will not here go into the significance of Jesus forgiving his sins, but the upshot was that Jesus said, '"I tell you, get up, pick up your mat and go home." While they all watched, the man got up, picked up his mat and hurried away.'

Jesus himself was astonished when he saw how much faith they had. There was mighty trust and confidence there. By their ac-tions they were really saying to him, 'We take it for granted that you can cure and want to do it. But we are going to make sure you do it.' And they went to great lengths to prove it.

The Roman centurion

Another good example of faith in the gospels was that of the Roman centurion who was especially praised by Jesus in Mt 8:5-13. He, a foreigner, asked Jesus to cure his servant who was dying. But when Jesus offered to come to his house, not wishing to inconvenience him, the centurion said, 'Oh no, sir, I do not de-serve to have you come into my house. Just give the order and my servant will get well. I, too, am a man under the authority of superior officers, and I have soldiers under me. I order this one "Go" and he goes; and I order that one "Come" and he comes; and I order my slave, "Do this!" and he does it.' When Jesus heard this, he was surprised and said to the people following him, 'I tell you, I have never found anyone in Israel with faith like this.'

What the centurion meant was amazing. Just as he, an officer, could command his soldiers and servants, Jesus could surely command illness and disease and death. He just had to say, 'Go' and the sickness would go. He recognised that Jesus had this extraordinary power.

So faith in the gospels is not just giving an intellectual assent to a list of truths. It is something deeper and more living. It is being convinced that Jesus can help us, that he wants to do it and that he will do it. It is a complete acceptance of the man.

Lack of faith

Now let us look at the opposite. The one thing that seemed to prevent Jesus from working miracles was lack of faith. Indeed, Jesus was greatly surprised by what he met in his own home town of Nazareth. At first the people welcomed him and were amazed at his preaching. But finally they rejected him. And Matthew says in a very telling sentence, 'Because they did not have faith, he did not perform many miracles there' (Mt 13:58). When I read that, I realised that Jesus was not just a machine who worked miracles when asked. Miracles were the outcome of a trusting relationship on the part of the suppliant. Indeed, much depended on the faith of the petitioner. If there was no faith there was no miracle. Indeed, those four words could sum it up very well: No faith, no miracle.

Besides, the miracle seems to have been in proportion to the faith, because Jesus often said something like this, 'Let it happen then just as you believe' (Mt 9:29).

We find, too, that Jesus was annoyed at the lack of faith of his disciples. After being with them for so long they still doubted.

Mk 4:40: 'Why are you frightened? Have you still no faith?'

I have always been amazed at the despairing outburst of Jesus in Lk 18:8: 'But will the Son of Man find faith on earth when he comes?'

Peter did not believe that Jesus would suffer
When Jesus spoke of his future suffering for the first time, Peter did not believe and began to rebuke him. He seemed to be saying, that is not the kind of messiah we are expecting. We want a triumphant not a failed messiah. Jesus' reply was very harsh: 'Get away from me Satan' (Mk 9:31-33).

Even after the resurrection it took the apostles a long time to believe.

Everything is possible with faith
Jesus himself actually said that 'everything is possible for the person who has faith.' Do you remember the scene where he said this? There was a boy who was possessed by an evil spirit that threw him about and physically injured him. His father brought the boy to Jesus because the disciples had not been able to drive the spirit out. The father said to Jesus, 'Have pity on us and help us if you possibly can.' Jesus' answer was astonishing, 'Yes,' said Jesus, 'if you yourself can! Everything is possible for the person who has faith.' The father at once cried out, 'I do have faith, but not enough. Help me to have more.' Jesus heard that cry and answered it in a dramatic miracle (Mk 9:17-29).

What Jesus was saying was, you yourself can do this, you yourself could work this miracle, if you have faith! It was the faith of the suppliant that made the miracle possible. What that boiled down to was a trusting relationship with Jesus. That was the key. Perhaps that is what Jesus meant when he said, 'if you have faith you can move mountains.'

Faith can move mountains
When Matthew tells this same story, he has a slightly different ending. 'Then the disciples came to Jesus in private and asked him, "Why couldn't we drive the demon out?" "It was because

you had not enough faith," answered Jesus. "I assure you that if
you had faith as big as a mustard seed, you could say to this hill,
'Go from here to there' and it would go. You could do anything!'" (Mt 17:19-21). I say to myself with astonishment, 'Is faith
that powerful?'

Faith not only in miracles
I am not really talking here about our having faith in Jesus'
power to work miracles. Faith is not only concerned with miracles. If it were we could be very self-centred, looking for things
for ourselves.

No, faith is a trust and confidence in God in everything. It is a
general attitude towards him. It is an acceptance of the fact that
he created me and put me here. He is interested in me. He has a
plan for me in life. And so everything that happens to me comes
from him. The good things, the bad things, they are all allowed
by God. And everything that happens is for my good. Even
when things seem to be at their blackest, he is still there caring
for me. I have trust, confidence in God in everything.

Faith in God
The real test of my faith would be if I could say to God, 'Dear
Lord, even if the worst thing possible came about, even if terrible things happened to me and to my family, even if I were a
failure in everything I did, even if I were accused of all kinds of
crimes, I would still trust you and know that all will ultimately
be for my good. No matter what comes I know that all will be
well and all manner of things will be well.'

That is the way St Alphonsus ends many of his prayers: 'Help
me to love you always and then do with me what thou wilt.' I
would love to be able to say that prayer and mean it. But I can't.
It would be too big a risk. Heaven knows what would come! I
hope that perhaps one day I will have that kind of faith, though I
know that is a gift of God.

We must have faith
I will be saved if I have faith. Perhaps, then, it is my lack of faith

that explains so much in my life. Is it the reason for all my failures? Is that why I do not advance in prayer? Is that why I find it
so hard to love certain people and even harder to forgive?
Perhaps most of us have not really accepted Jesus as a person
who is real and alive. Perhaps we do not really believe that he
can help us and wants to help us and will indeed help us.

If Jesus were to say to us, 'Do you believe I can do this for you?',
what would our answer be? Would it be a hesitant, doubtful
answer? Something like, 'Well, Lord, I am not too sure, but I'll
chance it anyway.'

Faith is about a relationship with Jesus and with God our Father.
We are saying, 'I trust you and I have confidence in you. I know
that you care for me. I feel absolutely safe in your hands. I will
try not to be afraid because I know all will be well.'

Consoling faith
There can be a consoling faith, a certain conviction that he is present, and at times a sense of warmth, that he holds me in his
arms. A sense of reassurance. I know I can rely on God *and* put
my trust in him. I feel confident.

Faith can bring great joy. The apostles felt this joy on Easter
Sunday night when Christ appeared in the supper room. It was
the same with the two disciples when they recognised Jesus in
the breaking of the bread. Mary Magdalene must have felt the
same joy at the tomb when the Risen Jesus said, 'Mary.'

Dark faith
On the other hand there can be the dark faith St John of the Cross
speaks of. In this God seems to have disappeared. He is no
longer present. He seems to have abandoned us. All is dark and
empty. There is no longer any joy in life. Indeed, life is not worth
living. At times we seem to reach the depths of depression. We
feel God will never return again. In this state, all one can do is
cling on in blind faith, trusting our faithful God. Many go
through this darkness. When it really hits, it can be terrible.
What keeps me going in this state is the realisation that this
could be God acting.

Christ experienced it in the garden, when he prayed, 'Father remove this chalice.' And again on the cross, when he cried out,
'My God, my God, why hast thou forsaken me?' For John of the
Cross, this is so much part of the spiritual life that it is to be more
trusted than the prayer of consolation, when God seems so near.

The Little Flower seems to have gone through this feeling of
abandonment towards the end of her life. Perhaps it was the
greatest suffering she went through. She too had to cling on with
dark faith.

There is a prayer we can all say frequently. It is the prayer of the
boy's father: 'I believe, Lord, help my unbelief.' Our faith and
trust can grow until we can say with St Paul, 'I consider it all as
mere refuse, so that I can gain Christ and be completely united
with him.' (Phil 3:8-9)

CHAPTER 8

The kingdom of God in the gospels

In 1967-68 I spent a year in Brussels doing a sabbatical in Lumen Vitae, the International Catechetical Institute. Towards the end of the year I had to do an exam for one of the professors. I told Fr Durwell, who was also a professor there, that I was doing something on the kingdom of God. He said, 'I advise you not to take that subject. It is too complicated.' Actually, it was too late to change, so I just had to go ahead with the kingdom. The exam was not great, but it went off well enough. Of course, I realise more than ever how complicated the kingdom of God is. The gospels present the kingdom in many different ways and they seem so disparate that I cannot grasp them. Yet I am sure there is a thread running through them all. So down the years, I have kept on studying the kingdom since I think it is essential for an understanding of Jesus. But I am consoled that not even the great scripture scholars can give us a simple comprehensive definition of the kingdom.

The central theme

The kingdom is generally looked on as the central theme of the synoptic gospels. Indeed, the word is rare in the other New Testament books. The Hebrew version is *Maluk* and the Greek *Baseleia*. Actually, the word does not mean kingdom in the sense of place or realm or domain. Rather it means reign or kingship. The term was familiar to the Jews in the time of Jesus, so he could use it without an introductory explanation. But it was less intelligible to the Greek-speaking Christians, and so it was little used in the rest of the New Testament when the message was addressed to them.

Use of the word in the Old Testament

The expression 'kingdom of God' is used only once in the Old Testament (Wisdom 10:10). However, in the Old Testament writings, God is everywhere called king. The Jews looked upon God as creator and so he was king of the universe. But he was their king in a special way. In the early days, the Jews had great confidence in their king. He had chosen them from among all the nations of the earth. He made a covenant with Abraham. He was their God and they were his people. Later he gave them the law of Moses to guide them. If they followed that law perfectly they would please God. Yet, in spite of trying to be faithful to the law, disasters befell them. They were even led into exile. There were foreign oppressors in their country. They began to wonder if God had forgotten them. Then in the Book of Daniel an answer began to appear. Daniel foretold that, sometime in the future, God would intervene on their behalf and liberate them. This would be prepared for by the coming of a messiah, who was described as 'A Son of Man'. With his coming, the kingdom of God would come. In the synagogues each week the Jews referred to this. They said, in the popular Aramaic, 'The kingdom of God is here'. So Jesus must have learned that expression in his boyhood.

Different ideas about the kingdom

As you can imagine, there were different ideas as to what kind of a Kingdom it would be. Some thought it would be liberation from oppression. Some thought it would be the restoration of King David's throne. Others expected a more spiritual kingdom. Others still thought that with the coming of the kingdom there would be all kinds of disasters. Some thought that the kingdom would come at the end of the world.

John the Baptist, too, spoke of the kingdom. He proclaimed that the kingdom was at hand. Then he spoke of someone who would follow him. This man would be greater than he and would baptise with the Holy Spirit and fire. The people were excited and eagerly awaited a messiah who would usher in the kingdom. They expected he would come soon.

Jesus' proclamation

Jesus lost no time after his baptism and temptations. He went around presenting his message. It was a simple and clear proclamation. 'The right time has come and the kingdom of God is near! Turn away from your sins and believe the good news!' (Mk 1:14). By 'The right time has come', he meant that there had been many stages in the history of the Jews. Now they were entering another stage. It was the last before the arrival of the kingdom of God. Jesus said it was 'near', it was approaching. He called on the people to accept this good news and repent. He wanted a radical change in their lives.

In his preaching he spoke often of the kingdom of God. The people were, as I have said, accustomed to the expression. However, Jesus never defined what exactly he meant by the word. Instead he told parables, or little stories, which often began with 'The kingdom of God is like ...' or 'To what will I compare the kingdom of God?' Then he would give a description of something the people were familiar with, or he told a little story. I have often tried, from reading the parables, to imagine what kind of a kingdom he was describing, but no single clear image comes across. These are some of the things he said.

The parables of the kingdom

Jesus speaks of the kingdom of God with the greatest enthusiasm. It was going to be a joyful time. It is like a wedding feast or a banquet. It is like the joy of a woman who found money she had lost. It is like the joy of a father whose wandering son has returned.

And this kingdom is so precious and so enticing that one would be ready to give up all in order to obtain it. It is the pearl of great price. It is the treasure a man finds hidden in a field and to get the treasure he sells everything he has.

The kingdom of God is something that begins small but then grows and grows. It is like the mustard seed, which is the smallest of seeds and yet grows into a tree. It is like the seed that is sown in good soil and brings forth thirty or sixty or a hundred fold. Like any seed, it grows quietly, without being noticed.

Everyone is welcomed into the kingdom, like the lost sheep or the lost coin. If anyone approaches the kingdom with repentance, the Father will run down the road to embrace and welcome the penitent. Indeed, the kingdom must be approached as a child, while, on the other hand, it is hard for the rich to enter.

Every type of person is invited into the kingdom, just as the net hauls in good and bad fish. Yet those who know that the great commandment is to love, are not far from the kingdom.

When I read all that, I felt it was obvious that, for Jesus, the kingdom was the most marvellous thing anyone could imagine. His enthusiasm reminds me of St Paul's quotation in 1 Cor 2:9.'What no one ever saw or heard, what no one ever thought could happen, is the very thing God prepared for those who love him.'

Why did Jesus use parables?

One of the great difficulties I had with the parables was Jesus' reason for using them. Jesus was asked that question directly. 'Why do you use parables when you speak to the people?' Scripture scholars are still puzzling over his curious answer. He said, 'The reason I use parables in talking to them is that they look and do not see, and they listen but do not hear or understand.' He then goes on to apply to them the prophecy of Isaiah: 'This people will listen and listen and not understand ... because their minds are dull and they have stopped up their ears and have closed their eyes' (Mt 13:10-15)

Is Jesus, then, deliberately trying to prevent some people from understanding his parables? It may seem that way at first sight. But another meaning is possible. Rather it is the attitude of his listeners that helps them to see or prevents them from seeing. Jesus soon discovered he had two kinds of listeners.

Those whose ears were closed

Obviously, there must have been people who were not interested in the things of God. On the other hand there were so-called 're-ligious' people, like the Scribes and the Pharisees. These were those 'outsiders' who were obdurate and hard-hearted. When they realised that Jesus was speaking of a new initiative from

God, they did not want that. They did not want new things. They wanted to have all as it had been in the time of their ancestors (Mk 7:5). Jesus was a threat to them, so they closed their ears. It was not Jesus who prevented them from hearing, but themselves.

They knew, of course, that Jesus was referring to them in some of his parables, especially the one about the rebellious workers in the vineyard who betrayed the trust of their master. Matthew leaves us in no doubt about this. He writes, 'Jesus said, "And I tell you the kingdom of God will be taken away from you and given to a people who will produce the proper fruit." The chief priests and the Pharisees heard Jesus' parables and knew that he was talking about them, so they tried to arrest him' (Mt 21:33-46).

Those who heard eagerly
On the other hand, there were many who heard his message with enthusiasm. These were people like Andrew and the disciples and those who followed him around. They had open minds and were striving for the kingdom. Everything Jesus said was full of meaning for them. They even came and asked Jesus to explain the parables to them. They were those who had something and to whom more was given. It was to them that 'the knowledge about the secrets of the kingdom of heaven (was) given' (Mt 13:11-12). They were the good soil bearing thirty or sixty or a hundred fold.

This distinction can apply to ourselves. If we are not interested in the things of God, we will not hear what Jesus is saying. But, if we are eager and want the kingdom of God and want it strongly enough, we will get it. To us, too, more will be given.

Is the kingdom present or future?
However, there have been many disputes among scripture scholars about the kingdom. For example, is it present here and now or is it something that will come in the future? A mighty debate has gone on about this for the past one hundred years. A couple of the sayings of Jesus seem to imply that the kingdom is

here now. Other sayings point to the future. Today the more favoured opinion seems to be this: The kingdom of God is approaching, but it is not here yet. It has begun and is growing and one day the fullness will appear.

There is a well-known phrase that sums it up, 'the now and the not yet'. The kingdom is here now, but it is not yet fully here.

Is the kingdom of God heaven?
Years ago many of us used think wrongly that the kingdom of God was heaven. This idea seemed to be confirmed by a part of the gospel we all knew well. It was the exchange, on Calvary, between the good thief and Jesus. 'Then he said, "Jesus, remember me when you come into your kingdom." He replied, "Truly, I tell you, today you will be with me with me in paradise."' (Lk 23:42-43).

Besides, the fact that Matthew always speaks of the 'kingdom of heaven' seemed to reinforce that idea. The kingdom was heaven. However, Matthew did not mean that the kingdom was only in heaven. He used the word heaven rather than God, because orthodox Jews never used the word God. And he was writing for the orthodox. So Matthew's kingdom of heaven has the same meaning as kingdom of God used by Mark and Luke.

Is the kingdom the church?
Years ago this was another simplistic idea we had. The kingdom was the church. And we were sure it was the Roman Catholic Church, because we thought that was the only true church! Even the other Christian churches were not the real thing. And as for the non-Christian religions, like Hinduism and Islam, they had not the true God. I am horrified now at our former arrogance.

No, the kingdom is bigger than the church, no matter how we define the church. Try to imagine two circles with the same centre, one bigger circle and one smaller. The bigger circle is the kingdom and the smaller is the church. They have much in common, but the kingdom embraces more. I have no doubt but that Hinduism and Islam are in the kingdom of God.

The social element of the kingdom
St Matthew, especially, brings the social element into our under-standing of the kingdom. However, Jesus did not lead a cam-paign to defend the rights of the poor and oppressed, as a mod-ern messiah would surely do. But when we look at the gospels carefully we see that he was concerned about their rights.

For example, we saw how he defended and helped the margin-alised, especially the tax collectors and sinners and lepers.

But one of the most dramatic things Jesus has to say about our social obligations is found in the last judgment scene in Mt 25. He tells us it is not sufficient to love our neighbour in the sense of accepting them as they are. We have to help them when they are in need and distress. In that scene, Jesus describes the Son of Man coming as king, sitting on his royal throne. Then he makes clear the conditions for possessing the kingdom. It is only if we feed the hungry, give drink to the thirsty, receive the stranger in our homes, clothe the naked, take care of the sick and visit those in prison, that we will receive the kingdom prepared for us. If we do not do these good works for our neighbour, we 'will be sent off to eternal punishment'.

Like the prophets of old
But in defending the poor and the needy, Jesus was not really doing something new. He was continuing the stand taken by the Old Testament prophets. They wanted what we would call today justice for all. They thundered out their message: to care for widows and orphans and the poor and the foreigner because they had no one to protect them; to give just wages to the poor and to give the wages in time; not to cheat when selling in the market place. Jesus was continuing that tradition.

In recent years we have become more conscious of the poor and the oppressed. The church has become the champion of their rights. The church has to help liberate those who are oppressed. Some scripture scholars see elements of this in Jesus' references to the unjust judge, to the unjust steward, to the labourers who had no work, to the cleansing of the temple. 'Blessed are the poor, for theirs is the kingdom of God.'

The kingdom and the new earth

Again in the beatitutes Matthew says, 'Blessed are those who are persecuted for righteousness' (justice's) sake, for theirs is the kingdom of heaven' (Mt 5:10). Righteousness (which is often translated as justice) means having a right relationship with others. We are righteous or just if we have right relationship with God, with ourselves, with our neighbour both as an individual and as part of society. Some would add that we should have a right relationship with creation as a whole. Nowadays, more than ever, we realise that there is a delicate balance in this complex intertwining of the different parts of the universe. Then the Bible tells us that sin came into the world and disturbed this balance and upset those relationships. Sickness has come and upset our physical and mental health. The ecologists tell us we have done our share in polluting the world by our exploiting of nature. All this is connected with the kingdom. And so the kingdom will come when we do our part to set that balance right. Indeed, those who fight for justice, and especially those who are persecuted for it, will find that the kingdom of heaven is theirs.

From all I have said it is obvious that this kingdom will be an earthly thing. How exactly it will work out we do not know. But it will be about this world and about people and our bodies and about justice. The imbalance we are familiar with will be set right. Then we will have the new heaven and the new earth.

But what is the kingdom?

I have been trying to gather some of the ways the gospels speak about the kingdom. But yet there must be a thread running through it all that gives us a meaning we can grasp. Can we now get any closer to describing what the kingdom is? From the things that Jesus said, I take it that the kingdom is bound up with a number of things. It is connected with his Father, whom he spoke of constantly. It is connected with his attitude towards other people. It is connected with our listening to the Good News.

CHAPTER 9

The kingdom: Jesus' vision of the Father

What comes across in the gospels is that Jesus saw life in a completely different way from other people. Above all, it is obvious that he had a tremendous sense of the sacred and the holy. God meant everything to him. The explanation given by some scholars is that Jesus must have had an extraordinary experience of God. When that happened we do not know. But obviously it must have happened before he started his preaching, because he had his message well worked out. However, there are a few incidents in the gospels that may be pointers.

The Jesus experience
St Luke (Lk 3:42) describes how when Jesus was twelve years old he was brought to the temple in Jerusalem. That was just a year before a Jewish boy reached manhood. Could that have been the equivilant of the *Bar mitzvah* we hear so much about in Jewish life today? Could it have been a celebration of his coming of age? And when he arrived, Jesus seemed to have been attracted to the Temple since he stayed on there listening and asking questions. And then there is his enigmatic question to Mary and Joseph, 'Did you not know that I had to be about my Father's business?' Could the experience have started here? Or had it already started?

Then at his baptism, after the Spirit had descended on him, a voice from heaven said, 'This is my own dear Son, with whom I am pleased.' Here there is mention of a deep relationship with God, that of Father and Son. And the Father was well pleased with the Son. Was that a peak experience for Jesus?

And again, during the forty days and nights in the desert, he was put to the test. And he proved himself. Resolutely, he refused to use his power as Son of God to feed himself or bribe others. He would not do something sensational like jumping from the pinnacle of the Temple, unnecessarily testing God's promise of help. He would not conquer the world by a short cut, rather than in God's way. On the contrary he would 'Worship the Lord (his) God and serve only him.' Once again he had confirmed his relationship with God. Could this have been the great and significant experience?

The Shema

What exactly his experience of God was, we do not know. But I wonder if it was connected with the *shema*, because every orthodox Jew was constantly hearing the *shema*. The *shema* was a few verses taken from Deuteronomy. We Christians are familiar with it from the gospel. The usual form is, 'Hear, O Israel, the Lord our God is one Lord; and you shall love the Lord your God with all your heart, and with all your soul, and with all your might' (Deut 6:4-5). The Jews were to keep these words in their heart. They were to teach them to their children. They were to recite them when they lay down at night and when they got up in the morning. They were to wear them on their foreheads as phylacteries. They put them on the doorposts of their houses in a *mezuzah*, a custom Jews still practise today. Indeed, Jesus could not get away from these words. They were being constantly drummed into his ears. And he also knew that, if he *did* obey this command, he was *assured by God* that he *would* be looked after in every way (Deut 11:13-21).

And another verse from the book of Leviticus was often added: 'but you shall love your neighbour as yourself' (Lev 19:18). Obviously Jesus had taken these ideas really to heart. Indeed, they became the basis of his whole preaching, to love God and one's neighbour too. And he wanted to obey the will of his Father in everything he did, because he knew his Father was looking after him. Now every practicing Jew knew the shema and recited it. So why was it that Jesus seemed to take this more seriously than others? I feel that a deeper realisation of the kind of person God is must have been the kernel of his experience.

Jesus and God

So the outcome of this experience was that Jesus had a remarkable way of looking at God. In Matthew 6 Jesus presents God in poetic language. He tells us that God cares for this beautiful earth which he created. He clothes the lillies of the field, and indeed all flowers, in beautiful garments. He feeds the birds of the air, so that they do not have to gather food into barns. Jesus saw him as a God who knows everyone and everything. He knows if even one bird falls from the sky, and there must be thousands and thousands of birds falling to the ground every year. And we, Jesus tells us, are more precious to God than many sparrows. This God cares for all people, not only for the chosen people. Does his rain not fall indiscriminately on the good and the bad? This God is gracious and compassionate, just as Jesus portrayed him in the parable of the Prodigal Son and in the parable of the vineyard owner who paid all his workers a full day's wages (Mt 20).

The wonder of this God overwhelmed Jesus. He fell in love with him. Indeed, he loved him 'with his whole heart and his whole soul and his whole mind', just as the shema said. God became the centre of his life. He saw God everywhere in the beauty of nature around him. He saw God in people who were precious. He sensed immediately that there was no need to worry, because God was constantly looking after him. Indeed, he so trusted God that he was ready to do whatever he wanted of him. This became his programme for life. 'My food ... is to do the will of him who sent me' (Jn 4:34). Naturally this changed his whole outlook on life and on every aspect of life.

This, then, was Jesus' vision of a gracious, caring and loving God. He found himself using one word to describe him. That word was Father. However, he used the more colloquial form, *Abba*. And his Abba had all the characteristics of a good father.

Jesus not only talked about his Abba, he spent hours praying to him. Above all he trusted him in everything. No matter what his Abba asked of him, he did it. Even if it were humanly difficult, even if he were asked to die, he said yes.

What did Abba want of him?
Jesus was so moved by the wonder of God that he was bursting to tell others. He wanted to shout it from the house tops. Like any one in love he wanted to tell everybody about his rapture. He obviously felt that if others could accept his vision of the Father, they, too, would be swept off their feet. They would love God. They would see life in a different way. But how was he to go about that?

As he approached thirty years of age, Jesus must have asked himself what plan Abba had for him. It is possible that his search for the will of God led him to the Jordan where John the Baptist was preaching. And when he arrived there, things did begin to happen. After he was baptised the Spirit descended on him. As Luke says, a new power, the power of the Spirit, came into him. Obviously he then knew what Abba wanted of him and his message to the world became clear.

He started to do the work his Father gave him to do. Luke describes it. "The news about him spread throughout all that territory. He taught in the synagogues and was praised by everyone" (Lk 4:14-15). He commenced giving the good news. Gradually, he began to see more clearly the plan of God for him. The Father had marvellous things in store for him. Something wonderful and terrible lay ahead.

God's plan for the world
But it did not stop there. God had a plan for the world also and it, too, began to unfold. Jesus told the people of this marvellous God he had grown to know. He wanted others to love him too "with their whole heart and mind and soul". He wanted to convey to them how God loved them because that was the foundation of his message. If they could accept that, the other part of

the shema would follow. They would love their neighbour as themselves. He asked them to accept others, to forgive others, to love others. This was to be the real sign of his followers: that they love one another.

This was his vision of a new world. It was obviously the dream of Abba for everyone. Jesus knew that Abba aspired to a world where tolerance, acceptance and love would be the bedrock of the whole structure. But it would be more than that. It would be something new, never before thought possible. It would be a world where conflict and war would disappear. Instead, people would be at peace and care for each other. It was the type of world Isaiah dreamed of: "They will hammer their swords into ploughs and their spears into pruning knives. Nations will never again go to war, never prepare for battle again" (Is 2:4).

So by accepting Abba and others, all would be transformed. The whole world would change. Creation would enter a new stage. This would be the time when life would be as joyful as a wedding feast. This would be a treasure worth selling everything for. This would be the most marvellous thing one could imagine.

He called this the kingdom
Again, Jesus searched for a word to describe all this. As I pointed out, he took a word all Jews were familiar with and that could support his vision. The word was the kingdom.

And so it was, as he left the Jordan after his baptism and his forty days fast, he knew exactly what he had to tell the world. He was going to tell everybody about his Father and the kingdom. For him the two ideas were intimately linked.

When I personally first had an experience of God, I had a little glimpse of what the Father is. I thought that that experience could be called the kingdom. 'The kingdom of God is within you.' Was the kingdom, then, the realisation that God was with me, was in me? In a way that is true, it may be one little aspect of the kingdom. But I think the kingdom Jesus describes is bigger than that. The kingdom is something that touches the whole world and all people. It is not merely a personal, subjective thing. Perhaps it starts as a little seed, but then it grows thirty, sixty, a hundred fold.

The in-breaking of God

I do not know who first described the kingdom as 'the in-breaking of God into the world', but I find it a wonderful description of the kingdom. God literally breaks into our world in a completely new way. True, he is already here upholding the universe and constantly re-creating it. He is present in every corner of it. He is present in each one of us. He is the ground of our being. But the new way he breaks into our world is that he is present through our awareness and acceptance of him. Jesus wanted all to have this awareness. He wanted all men and women to share his experience of Abba. He had this vision of a world in which all loved God with their whole hearts and minds and souls. He wanted more and more people to accept this God of his.

When people did accept his Abba, the in-breaking of God would begin. It would happen here and there in the midst of the cockle. It could emerge in this place or that place. Like the seed it would spring up during the night while no one noticed it. Its growing would be silent and gradual. Indeed, today, every now and then, I get sightings of it happening around us.

What Jesus seemed to be saying was that if enough people believed in this gracious Father as he presented him, then, automatically, the kingdom of God would be among us! There would follow the in-breaking of God into the whole of creation. God himself would be in every man and woman. All would accept God as gracious and loving. Like Jesus they would trust him in everything.

If all observed the Shema

Rabbi Levi, one of the old Jewish writers, said that 'if the Israelites observed one Sabbath as it should be observed, the Son of David would return immediately.' Perhaps we, too, could say that if all people followed the shema, by loving God and their neighbour, the kingdom of God would be among us. Is not that what Jesus implied to the teacher of the law?

Indeed, if everyone could accept that vision, everything would change. The whole world would change. The universe would change. For the first time, they would love God with their whole hearts and minds and souls. It would follow that they would love their neighbour. And then hatred and wars would disappear. There would be peace, not only in the hearts of each person but between nations. So by accepting God as Abba, all people would be changed. Everything would be transformed.

Our love of God

But let us wait a moment. It seems very simple to say that the kingdom of God will come when we accept Abba as presented by Jesus. It is not simple at all. What that would demand is frightening for us frail human beings. I often ask myself if I will ever come to accept God like that – as the most marvellous person that there is. Will I ever come to love God with my whole heart and mind and soul? Can God become the greatest thing in my life? Can he attract me more than the attractions of this world? I ask these questions, because our idea of loving God is strange.

A little incident may demonstrate this.

Can we really love God?

One evening, at a meeting with married couples, we were meditating on Jn 14:23-24. This is the passage: 'Whoever loves me will obey my teaching. My Father will love him, and my Father and I will come to him and live with him. Whoever does not love me does not obey my teaching.'

I asked the couples how we can love God whom we cannot see. One of the husbands explained to me that he loved God through loving his wife. I said surely there must be more than that. But he said that he did not think so. It was as if he said, loving God in himself is just not possible. All we can do is show a sign of it.

That I find hard to accept. Why, then, does Jesus talk so much about loving God our Father? Why does he demand that we love him, Jesus himself? Indeed, Jesus emphasised that one of the marks of being a disciple of his was to love him, even more than one's father or mother. Surely this must mean love as we humans understand it. I take it that Jesus is asking us to develop a deep affection, an attachment, a fondness for God and for himself. It seems to me that when the saints say they love God, they mean some kind of a deep warm feeling. John of the Cross writes so beautifully about loving God and describes it as the spiritual nuptials. It is like marriage. In his writings there is something passionate about this love.

I remember when my Christian Brother friend in Calcutta spoke of the love of God, I used feel a deep yearning and affection for this God who is the most beautiful thing there is. Often, in contemplation, one is swept into a sense of closeness to God and a sense of being loved by God and wanting to love in return. At times it can be like loving another human being.

So, I do not think it is sufficient, when speaking of the love of God, to settle for loving one's wife or one's neighbour, or doing one's work well, or accepting suffering. No doubt these are all signs of our loving God. But I know the love itself can be there.

That's the kingdom
So there it is. This is the kingdom! It is the in-breaking of God into our lives and into this world. It is that time when all of us will follow the shema and love the Lord our God with our whole heart and soul and mind. And loving our neighbour will follow from that too. The result will be peace and justice in the world. Even the whole universe will attain the freedom of the children of God.

Though the kingdom of God is God's doing, yet in a way, it depends on us. We can at least remove the obstacles. The way we can go about that is by accepting the Abba of Jesus. That means trying to get to know him. Then the kingdom has already begun in us. It follows that when more and more people accept God as loving, gracious and kind, the closer the fulness of the kingdom approaches. For us it means developing a great affection for God. It means utter and complete trust in him. It means being united with Jesus as the branch with the vine. It also means loving all men and women. It means fighting for justice for all, especially the oppressed. It means taking care of this earth of ours. And, when that comes about then the whole of life will change. Hatred will go and love remain. The fulness of the kingdom will have arrived.

CHAPTER 10

Discipleship

In the last five chapters I have been talking about getting to know the real Jesus, about having faith in him and about the kingdom. But a topic allied to these is discipleship. I find it is more difficult to present. The reason is that formerly we thought that what Jesus said about the cost of discipleship seemed too strict for ordinary Christians. As a result many of his sayings were applied only to religious. But now scripture scholars tell us the sayings on discipleship are meant for all Christians and not just an elite group. How did this change come about?

Formerly religious were looked upon as an elite group in the church. The religious life used be called 'a state of perfection'. That meant that when you became a religious, you could more easily reach perfection. In a word, religious could be holier! The reason given was that religious undertook many obligations beyond the call of duty. The ordinary Christian was bound to follow the ten commandments, but what made the religious life different was that, besides following the commandments, religious also bound themselves by the vows of celibacy, povery and obedience. So they followed the hard prescriptions of the gospels. They had to give up all they had to the poor and follow Christ. They had not whereon to lay their heads. They had to give up parents and brothers and sisters. They had to take up their cross daily and follow Jesus. They had to become eunuchs for the sake of the kingdom. They had to obey in everything.

Religious are not an elite
But scripture scholars tell us that you cannot argue from the passages about discipleship that the New Testament established a

special form of life for certain elite Christians. The call to discipleship goes out to all Christians. Besides, Vatican II changed this
idea. Chapter 5 of the *Constitution on the Church* (*Lumen Gentium*)
is called 'The Universal Call to Holiness'. In other words, all
Christians are called to holiness. In the same way, all are called
to discipleship.

Four hundred years ago Martin Luther stressed the same point
and stated it very forcefully. He said religious did keep the old
vision of the gospel alive. They left all for Christ's sake and en-
deavored daily to practise his rigorous demands. But by limiting
the application of the special commandments of Jesus to a re-
stricted group of specialists, the church evolved the fatal concept
of the double standard – a maximium and a minium standard of
Christian obedience, the religious and lay people. The result is
that we have presented the people with 'cheap grace', a watered
down version of Christianity (cf. *The cost of discipleship*, by
Dietrich Bonhoeffer, p 49-50). This cheap grace is the opposite of
what Luther called costly grace. It does cost to be a disciple of
Christ. While I found what Luther had to say disturbing, I saw it
as new and challenging.

Luther was right. We have taken the two standards for granted.
Not so much is expected of the 'ordinary' Christian. And so it
came as a shock to me that the severe demands of the gospels are
meant for all Christians. And if they were meant for all, I, as a
Religious, was even more strictly bound by them. So in practice,
this will mean looking at the sayings of Jesus anew to see how
they apply to everyone. By that I mean, where does giving up
possessions and leaving family and selling all for the pearl of
great price fit into the lives of 'ordinary' Christians? Today, I
think, all of us are challenged afresh to see where discipleship
fits into our lives.

First let us have a look at the gospels to see what Jesus has to say
about discipleship.

The gospel on discipleship
From the beginning of his ministry Jesus announced his pro-

gramme in the words of Mk 1:15: 'The right time has come,' he said, 'and the kingdom of God is near! Turn away from your sins and believe the good news.' Then he went around and called many people personally. They became his disciples. Now, what exactly did that mean, being a disciple of Jesus?

The meaning of the word 'disciple'
At the time of Jesus there were many groupings, religious and political, each with their own aims and way of life. In each group there were the masters and they had disciples. The Rabbis, St John the Baptist, the zealots and others had their disciples. Jesus followed this tradition.

In the New Testament the word 'disciple' is important. It is used two hundred and fifty times. The Greek word is *mathetes* and it means 'one who learns'. The disciple was an apprentice who attached himself to a master or teacher.

Not just one group called disciples
Part of our difficulty in describing a disciple of Jesus is that there was no set pattern of life for a disciple of Jesus. All were called to be disciples. Yet their ways of following Jesus were different. There were many different groups. These are the different groups Jesus gathered around him:

1. The twelve apostles, whom Jesus chose from among his disciples. They were a special group. They seem to have travelled about with him and stayed with him most of the time. They were with him on special occasions. They, alone, were with him at the last supper and in the garden at his arrest.

2. There were other disciples who also went about with him some of the time. Luke (10:1) speaks of his sending out seventy-two others, besides the twelve apostles, to preach the good news of the kingdom. Luke also tells us that, 'There was a large gathering of his disciples' (Lk 6:17). Indeed, Jesus speaks of wanting even more workers for the harvest. However, I have never seen any estimate of how many disciples Jesus had.

3. There were women who were part of the group. They provided

for the group out of their own resources and ministered to them. They, too, travelled with the group at times (Lk 8:2).

4. After that there were many friends and supporters who lived in their own homes but admired Jesus and followed his teaching. We read of Lazarus and his sisters Martha and Mary. There were Nicodemus and Joseph of Arimathea. There may have been many more of these admirers.

5. Finally, there were the multitudes on whom he had pity and who came to hear him speak. Many of them had great faith in him and followed him for days on end.

The disciples of Jesus were different

However, there was something special about being a disciple of Jesus. There were noticeable differences between his disciples and those of the Rabbis and of St John the Baptist and of the zealots. Noting these differences will help us understand what Jesus meant by being a disciples of his.

Jesus called each disciple personally

With other groups it was the disciple who chose the master or the Rabbi. Perhaps it was the same with the disciples of John. Jesus always personally called his own disciples.

From the beginning of his public life, we see him doing this. In the first chapter of St Mark's gospel we see the remarkable way he went about it. He was walking along the shore of Lake Galilee and he saw Simon and Andrew catching fish with a net and he simply said, 'Come with me, and I will teach you to catch men.' At once they followed him. A little further on he saw two other brothers, James and John, in their boat. He called them and again they, too, followed him immediately.

The call of Matthew, found in Mt 9:9, is equally surprising. As Jesus was walking along he saw a tax collector sitting in his office. He said to him, 'Follow me.' Matthew got up immediately and followed Jesus.

For Jesus the word 'follow' was important. In Greek the word is *akolouthein*, and it is used seventy times in the gospels. Perhaps the word 'acolyte' will help you to remember the word.

On the other hand, there were people who wanted to join Jesus but he would not accept them. Like the man from Gerasa whom Jesus told to stay at home and announce the kingdom to others. That was to be his way of following Jesus.

Jesus called even sinners and outcasts

Jesus did not restrict his invitation to the ritually pure and the religiously obedient. That, of course, was a strict demand in becoming a disciple of the Rabbis. Jesus, on the other hand, called all kinds. But he seems to have had a special predilection for the outcasts of society, those who were considered sinners by the pharisees. They are described in the gospels as 'sinners and tax collectors'. Jesus shocked the pharisees by inviting himself to dine with these outcasts, as, for example, with Zacchaeus. He carried on his well-known table-fellowship with them. He told parables indicating they were closer to God than the Scribes and the Pharisees. Even the prostitutes were closer to the kingdom of God. He was constantly inviting these sinners to be his disciples. What must have shocked at that time was that he had women among his disciples.

Jesus made extreme demands

This was not the usual teacher-disciple relationship. It went far beyond what the Rabbis or others demanded. Mark tells us that Jesus began his preaching with a very definite call: 'The right time has come and the kingdom of God is near. Turn away from your sins and believe the good news.' It was a call to a radical conversion and to believe the good news of the kingdom. What *did* this conversion entail?

a. It was a commitment to the man Jesus himself. It meant a complete acceptance of Jesus. Many of those who were called fell under his spell. I can imagine the disciple saying when he first met Jesus, 'This is what I have been looking for all my life.' The call of Andrew in St John's gospel is a good example of this. Andrew followed Jesus who invited him to come and see where he lived. He spent the rest of the day with him. It seems to me he left the house of Jesus stunned at what he had experienced and rushed off to tell his brother Peter, 'We have found the Messiah.'

The reaction of Nathaniel was somewhat similar. When Jesus told him he had seen him under the fig tree, Nathaniel burst out, 'Teacher, you are the Son of God! You are the King of Israel.'

Jesus expected this commitment from his disciples. He wanted faith from his followers. The way Jesus himself described this attitude towards him was to ask, 'Do you believe?' 'Do you have faith?' What he meant by that was, do you trust me, do you have confidence in me?

When many of his listeners left Jesus because his teaching was a hard saying, Jesus asked, 'Will you, too, go away?' St Peter cried out, 'To whom will we go? You have the words of eternal life.'

Jesus said he who is not for me is against me.

b. *Jesus demanded loyalty and love.* He demanded exclusive loyalty. 'If a person is ashamed of me and of my teaching … then the Son of man will be ashamed of him when he comes in the glory of his Father with the holy angels' (Mk 8:38)

And he demanded even more. One could not be his disciple 'unless he loves me more than he loves his father and his mother, his wife and his children, his brothers and his sisters and himself as well' (Lk 14:26).

The apostles seemed to have become more and more attached to Jesus as the time passed. At the end of the last supper, when Jesus told the apostles of his approaching death, Peter said, 'I will never leave you, even though all the rest do … And all the other disciples said the same thing.' I am sure they were sincere though, in the event, most of them ran away. Still they remained attached to Jesus.

c. *It was an acceptance of the vision and teaching of Jesus.* The vision Jesus had of the kingdom was centred around his Father. And so for him, the kingdom would be the time when all people would accept the kind of Abba he was presenting. I feel that this is perhaps what Jesus communicated to Andrew when they were first together. This vision Jesus tried to communicate in his preaching.

Of course, the kingdom meant even more than that. It meant accepting all his teaching and above all his message on brotherly love. This message is spelt out in the gospels. It was new and it was demanding. These are some of his demands: sharing everything one has; taking the last place; bearing insults and injury; constantly forgiving; never seeking revenge but loving even one's enemies and loving unto death if necessary.

Jesus demanded that they accept his vision and teaching. When many left him, Jesus did not change his message. Rather he insisted and said, 'Will you too go away?'

But, of course, accepting that vision was a slow painful growth. Only gradually did the disciples begin to realise who Jesus was. Even at the end of his life, they did not know why he had come. In Mk 8:29 Jesus asks, 'Who do you say I am?' Peter answered, 'You are the Christ.' To be able to say, 'You are the Christ', is a gift of God. Jesus told Peter that flesh and blood had not revealed that to him, but his Father in heaven.

d. *The disciple had to be ready to take up the cross.* When Jesus first spoke of his future suffering, Peter was shocked. That was not the kind of messiah Peter expected. He wanted a glorious, triumphant conqueror. But Jesus insisted, on three separate occasions, that he would suffer and then pointed out that they, too, would have to suffer. 'Whoever does not carry his own cross and come after me cannot be my disciple' (Lk 14:27).

Nowadays, they often refer to the cost of discipleship. Jesus tells us that this discipleship should not be undertaken lightly. One must sit down beforehand and work out the cost, like a man planning to build a tower, or going to war (Lk 14:28-31).

This is the costly grace Luther refers to.

e. Detachment from prized and cherished things. The call of Jesus changed the lives of his disciples. Jesus and the kingdom became the important thing in their lives. Everything else become less important. The disciple must be ready to give up even what is most prized and cherished. Here are some of the things Jesus mentioned:

* For all it was a call to turn away from their former life. Peter and Andrew no longer spent their time fishing. They went with Jesus to learn to be fishers of men. Matthew gave up his work as a tax collector. For some the change was not so external. It was an interior conversion.

* For all it meant suffering and the carrying of the cross for the sake of the kingdom. Jesus announced that he himself would have to suffer. His disciples must be ready to do the same. He insists on this. 'Whoever does not carry his cross and come after me cannot be my disciples.'

* For some it meant giving up their possessions. Luke tells us that Peter and Andrew pulled their boats up on the beach, left everything and followed Jesus. But Jesus made his most startling demand in Lk 18. He said to the eager rich young man, 'Sell all you have, give to the poor and come follow me.' That the young man could not do. He walked away as so many have done down the centuries.

Luke sums it up in the words of Jesus: 'In the same way, none of you can be my disciple unless he gives up everything he has (Lk 14).

But not everyone gave up all his possessions. For example Matthew followed Jesus but he still gave a big dinner next day in his house.

The women who went with Jesus used their own resources, which obviously they kept, to help Jesus and his disciples (Lk 8).

* For some it meant leaving their family. In Lk 14 Jesus speaks of the cost of discipleship. What he had to say on this point was

truly radical: 'Whoever comes to me cannot be my disciple unless he loves me more than he loves his father and his mother,
his wife and his children, his brothers and his sisters and his
life as well.'

* I am sure his Jewish listeners were horrified when Jesus said to
  a would be disciple, 'Follow me and let the dead bury their
  own dead' (Mt 22). To be with one's father in his final illness
  and to bury him was part of the Jew's piety to his parents. It
  was obvious Jesus intended to be radical.

* For some it meant following the poor itinerant life of Jesus.
  Jesus was constantly on the move and had no fixed abode. To
  the teacher of the law who wanted to go with him, Jesus
  summed it up well: 'Foxes have holes, and birds have nests,
  but the Son of Man has nowhere to lie down and rest' (Mt
  8:20).

* For all it meant sharing the mission of Jesus.
  Here again his disciples were unlike those of the Rabbis, who
  were students concerned with passing on the traditions of
  their teachers. The disciples of Jesus, however, were called for
  service. Jesus sent them out to heal the sick, to cast out demons
  and to proclaim the news that the kingdom of God was near at
  hand. Even those who did not travel with him had the same
  duty, like the man Jesus cured at Gerasa.

A summing up of discipleship
I think the words of Mk 3:13-14 are a good summing up of discipleship: 'Then Jesus went up a hill and called to himself the men
he wanted. They came to him and he chose twelve, whom he
named apostles. "I have chosen you to be with me," he told
them. "I will also send you out to preach, and you will have authority to drive out demons."'

l. They were chosen personally. 2. They were chosen to be with
Jesus. 3. And they were to be sent out on mission.

When one became a disciple of Jesus it meant a radical change. It
changed his attitude towards everything. Christ became the centre

of his life. It shaped his attitude towards property and wealth. It affected his human relationships. It gave a new meaning to love. It changed his understanding of success and personal fulfilment. And eventually, through his trust in Jesus, he entered into the very life of Christ and into his Paschal Mystery.

The early Christians
That is what being a disciple meant in Jesus' lifetime. After the resurrection, we find that the same pattern of discipleship continued. Instead of the relationship between the disciple and the flesh and blood Jesus, there was now a relationship with the Risen Christ. However, the word *disciple* is used only in the Acts. In the Letters, different words are used such as believers, saints, brothers. Under whatever name, being a Christian calls for this special relationship. Let us apply discipleship to our own lives.

What does discipleship mean in our lives today?
The disciple is called personally by Jesus. I think this could be looked on as a second conversion. It is not just the general call that comes with being born into a Christian family or by being baptised as an infant. I think this is a call later in life. A later conversion. Many people talk of this happening to them.

In detail, what does this call to discipleship mean for us?

a. It means commitment to Jesus
What do we think of Christ? Is he important to us? Has he become the centre of our lives? A conversion is primarily a conversion to God himself or to Jesus. It is a complete acceptance of Jesus. Has there been such a true conversion in our lives? I cannot truly call myself a disciple of Jesus, if I have not this commitment.

b. It means an acceptance of the vision and teaching of Jesus
Does the Fatherhood of God mean anything to us? Is the kingdom of God really the pearl of great price for which we are prepared to sell everything? Do we take seriously all the details of his message?

c. It means a radical change in our lives

It is a call to turn away from sin. It could mean turning away from many aspects of our former life. For each one of us, that means something personal and different. It could mean overcoming bad habits. It could mean living a life of prayer. Or, as with Matt Talbot, a life of prayer and penance. (Penance should be done only after consultation.)

It will certainly mean a willingness to suffer and carry our cross. Our own experience of living surely shows us that suffering is a part of life, not only for Christians but for every person. The important thing is how we react to it. Like Christ, do we carry the cross willingly, or do we grumble at every step? It is obvious that suffering is part of our following of Christ.

d. It may mean a detachment from things cherished

It could mean giving up things we are attached to. It could mean giving up some of one's wealth. It would certainly mean a spirit of detachment. It could mean living a poorer life style. It could mean giving up one's job. It could mean going to live elsewhere, or even abroad on the foreign missions. (I suggest that no one does any of these on the spur of the moment, but only after much thought and prayer and consultation.)

e. It means sharing the mission of Jesus

This could come about in various ways. Simply by praying more and attending Mass and the sacraments, or by being an apostle at one's work. By joining a political party. By getting involved in works of justice or social work. By helping out in the local church. Joining some lay organisation. Joining a prayer group or a handicapped children's group. Starting one's own group. It could mean becoming a priest or a religious or even a hermit! Each one has to find out for oneself.

PART IV

We begin to see ourselves in a new way

CHAPTER 11

The difficulty of accepting ourselves

I suppose we would all expect that seeing God and Christ in a new way would be part of conversion or transformation. But, as I pointed out, another important part of conversion is to see ourselves in a new way. Many find this difficult to understand. What has knowing myself and accepting myself to do with conversion? Perhaps an example of this from one of the parables of Jesus will help.

The Pharisee and the tax collector

'Once there were two men who went up to the Temple to pray: one was a Pharisee, the other a tax collector. The Pharisee stood apart by himself and prayed, "I thank you God that I am not greedy, dishonest or an adulterer, like everybody else. I thank you that I am not like that tax collector over there. I fast two days a week, I give a tenth of all my income." But the tax collector stood at a distance and would not even raise his face to heaven, but beat on his breast and said, "God have pity on me, a sinner!" I tell you, the tax collector and not the Pharisee was in the right with God when he went home. For anyone who makes himself great will be humbled, and everyone who humbles himself will be made great' (Lk 18:9-14).

Jesus chose two well-known types who were familiar to his listeners. The Pharisees were a rigorist group. They regarded all civil government over Israel as a usurpation, since God himself was their king. And so the law of Moses was the only law they recognised. They distinguished 613 precepts and they tried to follow them in the minutest detail. For them, salvation came through following these precepts perfectly.

The other character in the story was equally well known. Some tax collectors were chief tax collectors like Zacchaeus and some minor officials. In either case they were despised by the people for two reasons. They were working for the hated Roman conqueror and on top of that they were often unjust, probably by demanding excessive taxes. Like any people who are despised by their fellow country men, their lives were not exemplary. Indeed, most people grouped them with sinners. We read often in the gospels that Christ went to 'the tax collectors and sinners'.

The way the two men behaved in the Temple could not have been more different. The Pharisee stood apart by himself. He thought he was superior to others and his prayer expresses that. He thanked God he was not like others. They were sinners. Not only did he not sin, but he did good works. He fasted and gave a tenth of his income to the temple. He seemed to be saying, 'Dear Lord, you are fortunate to have someone like me to make up for all those sinners, like that tax collector over there.'

The tax collector, on the other hand, stood at a distance and kept his eyes down and beat his breast. It was the attitude of a man who was ashamed of himself. And his prayer, too, brought that out. 'God have pity on me a sinner.'

What intrigues me about the story is this. Why did the tax collector came into the Temple? I ask this question about him because it is obvious enough why the Pharisee came in. The good Jew, like the good Christian, went to 'church' often. And the Pharisee probably came to remind God how good he was. But the tax collector? In those days I am sure sinners were not in the habit of running to the Temple frequently no more than sinners today! So why did he come?

The only reason that makes sense to me is this: Something unusual must have happened. Perhaps he had committed a particularly big fault which pricked his conscience. Taking a cue from the Pharisee's accusations, perhaps he had been particularly unjust to someone. He may have ruined a farmer or a business

man. Or he may have committed adultery. He may have treated
some unfortunate woman in a degrading way, or he may have
got her into trouble. Or he may have tried to commit adultery
and been rebuffed. Whatever it was, it weighed heavy on his
conscience. He admitted his fault and did not try to deceive himself. He acknowledged he was a sinner. That drove him to God
to ask for mercy. I imagine if that something unusual had not
happened he would not have come to the Temple. He would not
have realised he was a sinner. He could not have prayed like
that. It was a good prayer because Christ praised him since he
went down to his house in the right with God.

I think it would be true to say that the Pharisee could never have
said the prayer of the tax collector. And why? He thought everything was going very well. After all, didn't he fast twice a week?
Didn't he give a tenth of all his income to God? What had he to
worry about? He was keeping the law perfectly. And not only
that, look at the sins he did not commit. He was not greedy. He
was not dishonest. He did not commit adultery. He committed
none of these sins. And that was perfectly true. Pharisees were
indeed like that. He had examined his conscience and discovered he had no sins. So there was no need for him to say the
prayer of the tax collector. He was all right and everything was
going well. He had no reason to humble himself before God.

St Luke tells us that the parable was directed at those who were
sure of their own goodness and despised others. 'Thank God I
am not greedy … like everybody else. I thank you that I am not
like that tax collector over there.' It never struck the Pharisee
that his prayer was a prayer of pride. Not only could the
Pharisee not say the prayer of the tax collector, but even God
could not get through to him.

What comes across to me from that parable is this. It takes something unusual to happen, something disturbing, to make us realise we are not in the right with God. We might then say, 'Oh I
wish God would send me "something unusual" like that. Then I
would be able to turn to him.' But the point is, God is constantly

sending things that will help us see our faults. These things are inbuilt in life and should shake us and disturb us. Unfortunately, like the Pharisee, we do not see them. They are too painful and disturbing and so we blind our eyes to them. It is only if we are shaken out of our complacancy that we begin to see. It is a painful awakening.

Lord that I may not see!

A example comes to my mind. Years ago when I was a young priest in Bangalore in South India, one of our fathers came to me one Saturday evening. He was preaching at all the Masses in the church at the weekend. He asked if I would listen to the sermon and tell him what I thought of it. I said I would. True to my word, I listened to him preaching at a few of the Masses. When he asked me afterwards, I remember saying that I thought the sermon was good. It was well divided and worked out and in-teresting. 'However,' I added, 'there were two small points that might help.' I told him he was inclined to drop his voice at the end of the sentences and that he could have changed his tone when starting a new idea. He looked at me with distain and said, 'I never drop my voice at the end of sentences.' I said, 'I have actually written down what I think are a few of the words I missed.' 'Not at all,' he told me, 'And about changing my voice, I changed at this place and that place.' I said, 'You may have but I did not notice it.' Again another look of distain. Before I knew he had raised his voice and was telling me about my sermons. Then he went on to tell all my other faults. I had to ask him to speak more quietly or everybody would hear him!

From that incident I learned two important lessons. One, never volunteer to tell anyone their faults! It is a mine field. Two, everyone is touchy about their own faults.

None of us wants to see our faults. Even if they are pointed out to us, we refuse to believe what we are told. I would like to go on to apply this to our own lives.

CHAPTER 12

What makes us tick?

What is going on deep within us? Why do we, like the Pharisee, find it so difficult to notice what is happening within us? When we do notice it, why do we find it so difficult to admit to ourselves that it is true? And why do we find it even more difficult to reveal it to others? These are the basic questions I want to deal with now.

The first question is, what exactly is going on deep within us? I think this is what Jesus is trying to explain to us in the parable of the sower. This parable is different from all the others in one way. Jesus tells it twice. He first tells the story, and then he tells it a second time by way of explanation. I will take Mark's version.

The parable of the sower

Jesus tells the story the first time in Mk 4:3-9. The sower scatters the seed. Some seed falls along the path. Some falls on rocky ground, some among thorn bushes and lastly some in good soil. A number of those who heard the parable came along with the twelve disciples and asked him to explain what he meant. So Jesus explains the parable. (This was probably an explanation to clarify a problem in the early church.) This is found in verses 13-20.

The seed is the word of God and the sower scatters the word. Now the word of God, or his message, is coming to us constantly. It comes in the ordinary events of everyday life. We are struck by something in a book or a sermon. We hear a remark someone made about us. A thought comes to us during a retreat. Some catastrophe happens in our life; we fall sick, a friend dies, we meet with failure. These are some of the ways Jesus sends us his word and speaks to us.

But, notice, Jesus now changes and uses the word 'seed' to describe different people. Some people, he says, are like the seed that falls on the path or on rocky ground. They soon forget about the word. Some are like the seed that falls among thorn bushes. Some people are like the seed that falls on good soil and these bear fruit.

What I would like to deal with here is the seed that falls among the thorn bushes. Notice what Jesus has to say about them: 'These are the ones who hear the message, but the worries about this life, the love for riches and all other kind of desires crowd in and choke the message, and they don't bear fruit' (vv 18-19). In other words, the thorns are so thick and strong that they choke the seed. We are prevented from hearing the word of God by 'worries about this life', by 'love of riches', and by 'all other kinds of desires' that crowd in on us.

Jesus tells us that these things so preoccupy us that they choke the word of God. Let us now have a closer look at what Jesus calls 'worries, love of riches and desires'. In practice, what are these things? In other words, what is going on within us?

What is going on within each of us?
I will deal with these three things in more modern language. They are fears, longings and needs.

I. *Fears:* There are fears bubbling away in us all the time, though we may not be conscious of them. Did you ever notice how often the gospels talk of fear? For example, 'they were terribly afraid'; 'they screamed with fear'. Or Jesus said, 'Fear not, it is I.' Fear is a primitive emotion that bubbles away in us constantly. The fears we feel can range from mild fear or apprehension and go right up to terror. For example, just going out in the car, giving a class, buying things, might cause mild apprehension. Have I brought all that is necessary? Will I be in time? And so on. On the other hand, I know a lady who has panic attacks. She can waken up in the morning covered in sweat, afraid to face the day.

We can fear different things. There can be fear:

* Of people. Some can be uneasy in the presence of certain people. It could even be real terror. Did you ever go into a crowded room and notice that one person stands out from the crowd? The room seems to be full of that one person you fear or who upsets you!

* Of situations. You hate a certain duty you have from time to time; you could be terrified to undertake a certain job; you may have to change to a new job and you are in a panic; you are changed to another place and you do not know how you will cope with it.

* Of illness. You feel a lump here or there on your body and immediately you think of cancer; you fear hospital or a heart attack; you dread the news that someone dear to you is seriously ill.

* Of the past. The thought of certain things we did in the past can cause us fear. We would hate if anyone knew about them. During a Journal Keeping weekend, a man told me the sweat ran down his back at the thought of some of his past actions.

* Of the future. The future can be frightening, because it is the unknown. What terrible thing does it hold in store for us? For example we could fall ill, we could lose our independence in old age and have to be looked after. We could see the gradual death of the companions we grew up with, etc.

* Of death. Many are terrified at the thought of death. They refuse to talk about it. More often it is the circumstances that will surround it rather than death itself that frightens us.

* Irrational fears. Some have a vague free-floating fear not attached to anything in particular. I suppose this is what depression is. These and other fears are always with us.

II. *Longings and yearnings.* We are always longing and yearning for something or other. The human heart is never satisfied. However, there are some basic things all of us yearn for:

* Acceptance. We have a deep need to be accepted by others.

* Recognition. We need to be recognised for something that is unique to us.

* Belonging. There must be a place or a group of which we are a part.

* Love. We all need to be loved. If anyone feels he is not loved, it can have a devastating effect. It can lead to destructive behaviour. This is one of the deepest longings we have.

* There are sexual urges. In former days we did not speak openly about these. But they are in us all because we are sexual beings. Sex is a strong appetite. A lady told me she did not know why there was so much talk about sex, until it struck her! Then it was like a volcano!

* Ambition to succeed can be strong in some. They will stop at nothing to achieve their aim.

* Jealousy and need for revenge at hurt feelings can lead us to terrible lengths.

III. *Needs.*

1. There are the basic physical needs that are part of being human and having bodies. We need food, drink, warmth, shelter, clothes. In our affluent society we take these things for granted. But during the war some who were prisoners in concentration camps tell us that when starving, they thought of nothing else but food. Indeed, at times they were ready to kill for it. We have all seen films of the starving people of Ethiopia, looking like skeletons, yet walking for miles to get something to eat.

On one occasion, I was doing a course and part of it was a 'desert day'. That was a day when we were on our own and could go where we wanted. Some went off for the day and took some food with them. Some even fasted. Since I had not fasted for a long time, I decided to try it. I had a cup of coffee early in the morning and a few times during the day. At night I had a cup of tea and went to bed. I was amazed at how easy it was. That is until until I woke about three in the morning starving! I had to go to the kitchen and get something to eat. It brought home to me that the body has its own laws and we have to pay attention to them.

2. There are created needs that come when the basics are supplied. We are all familiar with these. We want parties, amusements, a good time. We want comforts and fine clothes. And what lengths we will go to to get them.

A young teacher in Dublin told me she was teaching very young children. Each evening after school, she was so tired that before she even prepared a meal, she would have to rest for a while. She was more tired as the week went on and was exhausted by Friday evening. What amazed her was this: If she were going to a dance or a party at the week-end, she could go around the shops looking for a dress on Friday evening. Where did she get the energy? It was obvious there was a deep need there.

Men, as well as women, like nice clothes and nice things! But men are often more interested in things like cars, gadgets, computers and radios.

If you have done much reading on these matters, you will notice that these three divisions are loosely based on Abraham Maslow's well-known Pyramid or Hierarchy of Values.

How we react to these fears, yearnings and needs
Now all these fears, yearnings and needs are bubbling away constantly. We do not notice them until something touches our fears, thwarts our yearnings, or deprives us of our needs. Imagine that you had three open wounds on your arm, so painful that if you touched any of them you would jump. Well, there are three very sensitive psychological areas within us, called fears, longings, and needs. So long as they are not touched we are hardly aware of them. But then if someone touches them, it is like touching a boil or an open wound. We jump.

I remember before I went to India, I had to get a primary vaccination against small pox. I had not been vaccinated as a child. In a short while my arm became swollen and sore and sensitive. I could not touch it. Then one day someone came behind me and caught me by the arms. I could have screamed with the pain.

Now imagine that we have these three psychological, open wounds. They are tender. If these areas are touched, we jump. And how! We ourselves may be surprised at the vehemence of our reaction. Often it is out of all proportion to what has happened or was said or done. I am sure you have often heard someone make a seemingly innocent remark about some one in the group, and unexpectedly the target of the remark becomes very angry. You did not expect a reaction as violent as that. Obviously, something deep within him has been touched and it hurt.

Different reactions

These are some examples of my own and others' reactions. We become angry or even aggressive. It is possible we could even strike someone. Or we refuse to talk. We stamp out of the room. We become jealous. We plan revenge. We complain and make cynical remarks. Or we react in a completely different way. We overeat or overdrink. We feel frustrated and depressed. And all this because some sensitive part deep in us has been touched and hurt. Like any wound it takes time to heal. I am sure each of us recognises some of these reactions. Which would be our way of reacting?

I like to put it in a melodramatic way: 'If I scream at you, I am really screaming at myself!'

Psychic energy

Carl Jung talks about psychic energy. I used wonder what that was. Now I think these reactions I have described are an example. We are going along peacefully, and unexpectedly our fears or longings or needs are touched. Then there is that sudden rush of anger or aggression or jealousy. It surges like a mighty storm. There is tremendous energy in it. This is psychic energy. The mystery is, where did it come from?

An example of how we react

A nun told me that she was a good friend of her superior. But one day the superior offended her. After that she noticed that every time she met her she deliberately gave her the cold shoulder. She told me it was like looking down on the scene from above. She could see herself walking along the corridor and her superior coming towards her. Then she would look the other way and walk past her. She knew how childish it was, but she could not stop herself! There was a dreadful compulsion in it.

Coming to terms with our fears

These fears and yearnings and needs are never satisfied. They continue bubbling away. The most we can hope for is to keep a certain balance. If not, they could lead to compulsions, mania and neuroses. I suppose maturity is coming to terms with these things that will always be there and frequently take us by surprise. Likewise, it demands that we have a lot of tolerance towards those who react in this unexpected way. Most people can control these things sufficiently to get on well enough in society.

Some, however, have king-size fears and yearnings and needs. Their reactions are not only unpredictable but often violent. They explode very frequently. As a result they can become very depressed. They feel all are against them. They cannot live at peace in society. Often they can be dangerous. These people need help. But it is not easy to suggest that to them. If you have ever had to try to get someone to go for psychiatric help, you know what I am talking about. And yet, getting psychiatric treatment is quite common today and has lost much of its terrors. But still!

A great obstacle to the spiritual life

These reactions can be a great obstacle to the spiritual life. They so preoccupy us that we do not hear the word of God. This is the main conclusion I want to present so I will deal with it in the next few chapters.

CHAPTER 13

The great obstacle to hearing God

Here is a short summing up of the last chapter: When our fears and yearning and needs are touched we react. Our reactions are like the thorns that choke the seed, so we do not hear the word of God. The reason is we are so preoccupied with the hurts that we hear little else. Even God himself cannot get through to us. This is one of the great obstacles to advancing in the spiritual life. The truth of this has gradually been coming home to me over the years.

Some years ago, I did a course in Spiritual Direction. At first I thought we would spend most of our time studying different schools of spirituality, the many ways of praying, scripture to help others pray from the Bible, and some theology. Of course we did all these subjects. But most of our time was taken up with noticing what is going on within ourselves.

A classic case

Here is a typical situation we have all met: Someone comes to us to pour out his troubles. We discover that he is angry or hurt or unhappy or frustrated. We realise that at this point there is no use talking about God. It is not that there is any ill-will on his part, but he would not hear us if we spoke about God. We have to deal with his problem first. The hurt, the anger, the frustration is so urgent and so immediate that he can give his attention to nothing else. At the moment, he is living in a closed world of his own pain and suffering. Nothing can break into that closed world. God has no chance of attracting his attention. He cannot hear God. For some time, deep, calm prayer will be impossible or, for that matter, prayer of any kind. The immediate problem must be solved first.

Another case

Or it could be that he is yearning and chasing after his desires. He has set his heart on that job, or that car or winning that golf tournament or that woman. To obtain that is the goal of his life at the moment. All his thoughts are on that. We can become infatuated, not only with a woman or a man, but with things too. I often find myself in that state. There is something I am engrossed in; it could be a computer or some work or a holiday I am planning, and I can pay attention to nothing else. I often meet others so immersed in seeking things that they are oblivious of the needs of those around them. Here again, even God cannot get a look in. We just cannot hear the word of God.

What the spiritual masters say

What I have just come to notice in myself and others, some of the great writers discovered centuries ago, as you can well imagine. However, these writers use their own particular imagery. Here are some examples:

* St Paul discovered that surprising things were going on within himself. He describes it very well in Romans 7. He says, 'I want to do what is good and I find myself doing what is evil.' In other words, no matter how strongly I want to do good, I find there is another force within me that wants to do evil.

* St John of the Cross, too, describes this in his own way. While he is giving us an excellent picture of the development of the spiritual life, he takes about seven chapters to describe all the things that absorb us. This is in the first book of the *Ascent of Mount Carmel*. He calls them the appetites. He tells us that the appetites torment a man, fatigue him, dull his mind. They are like children whining to their mother for this and that and are never satisfied. (*A.M.C. I*, Ch 6). I think that is a marvellous description of the fears and longings and needs I find within myself.

* Joannes Tauler also calls them appetites. He uses unusual imagery. He says the appetites encrust us and they are so tough they are like a bear skin. Even God cannot penetrate them.

The big question

The question I would like to ask now is this: How can we, in any crisis, eventually cease being absorbed with our fears and our yearnings and our needs? How can we get to the stage of being able to stand back and look at ourselves and see what is really going on within us? I ask that question because it is only then that we will be free enough to hear the word that God is constantly addressing to us. If only we could get that breakthrough, just as the tax collector experienced in the Temple. Well, that is a long, long process. As a preview, I will give an example that sums up the process.

An example of the process

I can sum up all I have been saying in a story that I tell against myself. I was Rector of our house in Dublin at the time. One day before lunch, I was rushing to finish off some work before leaving to stay with my mother in Belfast. A rap came to my door and in came a father with whom I was working very closely. He finished his business and before he left he remarked to me, 'There is one thing about you that annoys me very much.' I told him I'd be pleased to learn a little more about myself. And I meant it. At least I thought I did! Now I had better explain my method of working at the time. When I was at home, and not out on missions, I was very busy. I would receive letters or phone calls asking for priests to give a mission here, do a supply there, hear confessions in some parish and so on. I knew there was little chance of contacting men immediately, so I used make a note of the work and slip it into my back pocket. The time I was more sure of meeting the members of the community was at meals. Then I would produce my note and ask this man or that man about doing some job. The father who came into my room that day did much work in the house and much outside. He, too, was busy. So he said, 'You often come to me and ask me about some work when I have just returned to the house and I am not psychologically ready.' I thanked him and said I'd see what I could do about it.

Then I finished my work. I threw some clothes into a case and had a hurried dinner. Then someone drove me to Amiens St station. When I got into the train, I put my case on the rack and sat down. It was the first time for hours I was able to relax. But what was the first thing that came into my head? It was what that man had said to me, of course. I had been happy when he told me his complaint. But now the injustice of it all hit me. 'He was not psychologically ready!' What nonsense! Nobody ever comes into my room, or the room of any superior, and asks, 'Are you psychologically ready to listen to me?' Not at all. Most people come into my room and just start off without even asking if I am busy. Some can go on for hours. They leave when they feel they have said what they want to say. And so, racing around in my head was the phrase 'Psychologically ready!' By the time the train reached Drogheda, twenty-five miles away, I was at white heat. I was planning what I would do. I'd type out a note, 'Are you psychologically ready to listen to me?' And I would write it in big letters! I'd present it to him the next time I had to ask him to do some work. That would show him! I was still furious when I reached Belfast. But a few days with my mother helped to calm me down. Eventually I was able to tell that story to the man concerned. We still joke about it.

Did you notice the process that went on within me, during this incident? Perhaps not. Indeed, when I was going through it, I did not notice the details. However, later on when I looked back on it, I could see the different stages clearly. And so in the next chapter I will outline the stages of the process.

CHAPTER 14

The stages of accepting ourselves

God is constantly speaking to us, yet we do not hear him. Why? So often, the seed of the word of God does not bear fruit in us. Why? I was trying to give at least one answer to that question in the last chapter. If only we could notice what is going on within us and begin to accept that that is the way we are, we could begin to do something about it. But we find it difficult to accept these weaknesses.

St John the Baptist and acceptance
Years ago I was struck by a passage from St John's gospel, Jn 3:25-30. The John mentioned is, of course, John the Baptist who was on the east side of the Jordan preaching and baptising. He was the popular preacher of the time. Many people of all classes were coming to him. Then a young man called Jesus came and was baptised by John. Soon, Jesus himself started preaching. John had many disciples and some came to him to tell him that Jesus was now baptising and everyone was going to him. I imagine the disciples were anxious. They may have been asking them-selves, 'Is John now losing his popularity? Will all the people gradually drift away to Jesus? Is it wise to stay with John?' Perhaps they were hoping for some reassurance from John and that he would say to them something like, 'Now, do not worry about the people leaving us. Other preachers have come and gone, but the people still come to me. When Jesus has gone they will still come to me.' At least, that is what I would have hoped to hear from him.

But John did not say anything like that. In fact he said the very opposite. I'll take the translation from Ronald Knox's version,

which is striking: 'John answered, "A man must be content to receive the gift given him from heaven and nothing more."' In effect he was saying, 'I am me and I am content to be me. I have
been given a job to do and I am content with that. I am not the
messiah. I am only the messenger sent ahead of him. When my
time is over I will go. I have no ambitions. I am content to be
what I am.' Just listen to John's actual words again: 'A man must
be content with the gift given him from heaven and nothing
more.' John was content with the gift God had given him. He
was content to be himself.

Most of us are not content to be ourselves. We would all like to
be better. Especially do we find it difficult to admit some of our
faults. Indeed, we would die of shame if others knew them. We
try to hide them. And we may even be afraid to discover more
faults in ourselves. This can be a real fear.

I'd hate to know more about myself
I was giving a retreat to nuns in Wexford. During the retreat
there was a conference for teachers going on in the town. Some
nuns of other orders were staying in the convent for the conference. One of them asked me if she could attend the retreat when
she was free. I said of course. She came a few times. After a couple
of days she came to tell me she was leaving and wanted to say
thanks. And then she added, 'There is one thing I am afraid of. I
would hate to know more about myself. I do not know what I
would discover!'

This may come as a surprise to you, but getting to know ourselves and accepting ourselves can ultimately be a satisfying experience! However, it is a long painful process. It is like facing
death and it is indeed a kind of dying to ourselves.

The stages of physical death
Dr Elizabeth Kübler-Ross is a doctor working in Chicago with
the terminally ill. She established a seminar to examine the
stages people go through when they are dying. In her book, *On
Death and Dying*, she concluded that people who are dying go

through different stages. Here is a brief summary of her five stages:

1. *Denial and Isolation.* When the patient is told he has a terminal illness his first reaction is denial and refusal to accept this news. He thinks, 'There must be a mistake; The X-rays got mixed up; I'll get a second opinion.'

2. Then the patient begins to feel *anger.* He is angry with many people – doctors, nurses, relations, God. 'Why did God allow this to happen to me?' 'The doctor did not look after me.' 'Nobody understands.' He did not expect his life to be cut off so unexpectedly.

3. Then he begins *bargaining.* A gleam of hope comes. The end could be postponed if promises are made. This bargaining is usually made with God and usually kept secret or mentioned only to the chaplain. It may be a promise to make up for past neglect. It could come from a sense of quiet guilt for not attending church and should not be dismissed too easily. Some promise parts of their body to science.

4. *Depression.* The depression comes quickly enough. After all he is in the process of losing everyone and everything he loves. He may be worrying about who will look after dependents. If he is allowed to express his sorrow his final acceptance will be much easier.

5. *Acceptance.* When does this come? A few patients may fight to the very end. But most, if given enough time to work through the previous stages, will reach a stage during which they are neither angry nor depressed about their fate. A typical patient will have been able to express all his emotions, his anger and depression. He will have mourned his impending loss. He now contemplates his coming end with a certain degree of quiet expectancy. There has come a time for the final rest before the journey. Usually it is the family that needs more help at this time.

Through all these stages most patients had hope up to the very end. There may be some new treatment or a new drug that gives them a sense of mission. They show great confidence in the doctors who give them cause for hope.

Our death to ourselves

How does all this apply to accepting ourselves? When we have to face up to ourselves, we go through more or less the same process as Dr Kübler-Ross described. It is the process of dying to our weaknesses and our faults. It is a painful struggle. It may be a long time before we come to acceptance. Yet it is gradual and has to be worked through step by step. The stages are similar.

The stages of acceptance of ourselves

* The process begins when we learn things about ourselves. This can happen in many different ways. Someone points out a fault I never suspected; someone makes a hurting remark; someone accuses me in anger; something I read in a book strikes home; a point I hear in a retreat describes me; my director points out something unpleasant; or something just strikes me. Whatever way it comes, it takes me by surprise.

* Then I *deny* it. I refuse to believe it. My reaction is, 'I am not like that. That is so unfair.' Or I say, 'I am not that kind of person.'

* Then I begin *excusing* myself. I am not responsible for the things that have happened. Later I start blaming others. They did not do their part. They did not help me.

* I become *angry*. I may even feel bitter because I think I have been badly treated. I may begin planning how I will prove I am right and others wrong. I may even plan how to get even with others. Our fantasies often run riot.

* I feel *depressed*. Nothing will ever go right again. All is black. It is the end of the world. I may even feel, in this depression, that nothing worse could have happened. There is no hope for the future.

* *Bargaining*. This is one of Kübler-Ross's stages which I have not experienced in myself. I could be wrong about that of

course – perhaps I am deceiving myself! However, I mention it because others might recognise it right away. I remember a humourous story that may be an example. A Redemptorist was waiting in the sacristy to go out to preach a sermon. He was always very nervous before a crowd. Someone heard him offering a prayer: 'Oh, God, if you help me through this sermon, I promise I'll be a good priest!' Again, perhaps doing penances and going off things for Lent or saying extra prayers is a kind of bribery or bargaining.

* Then usually the anger and excusing oneself and blaming others continues for a long time. It is a painful period. Indeed, if the person is very sensitive, it can be dreadful. And yet the process cannot be short-circuited. It must be worked through, stage by stage. Of course, the length of time this distressing stage goes on differs with each individual.

The outcome – acceptance

Hopefully, then, after a longer or shorter period, I may be able to accept and say 'yes' to my faults and limitations. I may be able to admit, 'Yes, that is me. That is what I am really like.' At the same time I come to realise it is not the end of the world. An alternative way of facing life begins to appear, and there is a new hope. Gradually, I see I have come through the ordeal successfully. I should now be a better person because I know something more about myself. Usually there is a tremendous relief and even joy at giving up the useless struggle. Would to God we could all reach that stage!

A danger: Getting stuck in anger

Acceptance may not come as easily or as quickly as I have described. There is a danger that I may get stuck in anger. As a matter of fact this happens very often. It usually takes a long time for acceptance to come. At least that is the way it is with me!

From watching myself and others, I notice that we often continue to seethe with resentment. We persist in trying to defend ourselves. We get new ingenious ways of blaming others. Often we become so hurt with this humiliation that we cannot do our work properly. We are distracted at prayer. Indeed, prayer is almost impossible as long as we are in this state. Perhaps we succeed only in making ourselves miserable. And worst of all, we can make others miserable too, though I do not think everyone does that. At least this is something I, personally, try to avoid. In any case, this anger can go on and on. Indeed, I have seen it going on for a life time with some. They became angry, bitter people.

It is sad to meet people who go this way. We all know them. They go through life with a chip on their shoulder. They get angry at the least provocation. They can even get into black humours. They try to convince us and themselves that losing their temper is a good thing. 'It clears the air,' they say. However, others around them are never sure whether they will find them in good form or bad form. Their companions wish it were one or the other. I often wonder if they themselves are unaware of their own moodiness.

Angry for life

I met a good example of this some years ago. Once on a mission in a small town, I was visiting the main street where the shops were. I came to one of those old-fashioned banks, where the bank was on the ground floor and an apartment for the bank manager's family above. I called at the side door and met the manager's wife. She told me her husband would come up when he was free and then she said, 'I'd better warn you. I do not know how he will take you.' Then she told me the story. Years earlier when they were getting married he was hoping for two things – he wanted promotion and he hoped to be changed to a certain place. He got neither. She told me he had since got his promotions and that they had lived in lovely places and even in the place he had wanted to go to. But he never forgot his disappointment. He talked about it often and could still get angry and bitter about it. He took it out on his wife and the family. He was impossible to live with. She told me all the children had left as soon as they went to university. He was still an angry and bitter man. Actually, when I met him, he received me well.

However, I was convinced that his anger and bitterness must have had its origins well before the time of his marriage. Now, whether he changed after our meeting I never heard. But I doubt it!

Anger from a temporary situation

We often meet people whose anger lasts as long as the situation causing it lasts, and this is quite common. For example, someone may be doing a certain job or working with certain people. There is something about the job or about his co-workers that he cannot accept. Or it may be a bad marriage or a drunken spouse or a bad neighbour. He may be angry nearly every day as long as the provocation is there, but when the job is over or the annoying co-worker or bad neighbour goes or the drunken spouse dies, he gradually returns to normal. The problem solves itself. But while he is going through it, the pain from the situation is great. And he may take it out on others and be hard to live with.

How can we escape being stuck in anger?

There is no doubt that on every occasion we have to face ourselves, we spend sometime in the period of refusal, denial, blaming others and excusing ourselves. What is it that could help us to get out of that crippling and unproductive period? Is there any way of shortening the time in which we come to acceptance? I would like to suggest a few possibilities from what others have told me and from my own life.

CHAPTER 15

Becoming unstuck from our anger

On the way to acceptance, we often get stuck for a very long time in anger. Indeed, we could get stuck in it for life, an unfortunate situation. More usually we get stuck for some time. But often it is an unnecessarily long period which is crippling and unproductive. What I would like to discover is this: is there any way we can become unstuck from our anger more quickly?

Let's try to work it out
Kübler-Ross is not much help here. Indeed, she does not give any indication as to how one comes to acceptance. She just says that acceptance comes. Nor have any other books been of much help. However, I know it happens that people can become unstuck from anger without having to spend a long time there. So I will give some examples of where it seems to happen. These are based on my own and others' experiences. Perhaps I may eventually get to the principles behind it all.

a. An atmosphere of friendship, acceptance, love
I feel that if we had the right atmosphere, it would help. I mean, if there is an atmosphere of friendship and acceptance and love, whether in community, or in the home, or among friends, we would experience the support that would help us face the truth about ourselves. Here is an example:

He could not accept the humiliation of it
One evening I was in a religious house, as a visitor. At supper I was sitting opposite a priest I never met before. He was doing a postgraduate course and staying in the house. After the meal he asked me if he could speak to me and I invited him to my room.

His story was this: He was obviously an educated and intelligent man, but he was not accepted by his community. This depressed him. Through his work, he came in close contact with a woman who was working in the house. She accepted him and he found he could talk to her and pour out all his troubles. He was good with his hands and he used go to her house and do a lot of building and repairs. He gradually fell in love with her. One of his superiors told him very gently that there was a lot of talk in the community about the relationship. Another member of the community was equally kind, but others shunned him, in spite of all he did for the community. That drove him more into the arms of the woman.

Then people outside began to gossip too. Eventually, he felt he either had to give her up or marry her. He could not give her up. He still kept defending himself. The community did not even try to undersatand his situation. She was the only one who could give him the support the community did not give him. But I began to notice a change. He admitted he would not be happy if he married her, and yet still felt drawn to her. The image I had was of a man sliding down a steep slope, just hanging on by his fingers tips. I called to see him some weeks later in his own house. Most of his community were still giving him the cold shoulder and he could not talk to them. However, his superior and a few others continued to be kind. Yet, he was still attracted to the woman. It was touch and go whether he would stay or leave. The choices seemed to be: marry her and both of them be unhappy, or stay on and be unhappy anyway. Later I heard he had left that house and had gone to another place. Obviously, he had decided to get away from the woman. I have since heard that he has returned to his religious congregation.

I felt that the one thing that kept him from entering into what he knew would be a disastrous marriage was the willingness of his superior and a few confrères to listen to him and show him kindness.

So would I be right in saying an atmosphere of acceptance and

understanding could help us get through a difficult period like
that? Sandra?

b. *To talk about the problem is a well recognised solution*

However that is often the one thing we cannot do – talk about it.
If the problem hurts us very much we cannot run the risk of
telling others. Some years ago there was a popular book on the
subject called *Why am I afraid to tell you who I am?* It is by Fr John
Powell, an American Jesuit. It is a wonderful name for the book.
It is asking a very basic question. Why do I find it so hard to talk
to you about what is deepest in me, about my worries and my
failures and my weaknesses? His answer is this: 'It is all I have
and you may not like it.' So if I tell you what is deepest and most
vulnerable in me, and you reject me, I could not bear that. The
shame would be too great. And so I will not run the risk. I will
not talk about it. I will not tell you who I am.

However, it makes a great difference if we have someone we *can*
talk to. It could be a friend or a confessor or a spiritual director. It
must, of course, be someone who is willing to listen. I think the
following story is a good example of how being able to talk can
help:

At last she talked

I was doing a course, part of which was a 6-day directed retreat.
After the six days were over we met to share our experiences.
Each in turn talked about what the retreat meant to him or her. It
came to a nun I knew very well. She started to talk, but after a
few sentences she burst into tears and sobbed. The group was
wonderful. They said nothing and eventually she sobbed herself
out and composed herself. Then she continued. I remember
clearly what she said: 'This retreat is the first time I have realised
how much I resent being a superior.' She was superior in her
community although she was the youngest member. She felt
others expected her to be a certain type of person and to act in a
certain way. As a result she could not be herself and she felt stif-
led. It was only during that retreat she discovered this was her
problem and the dam burst. It all poured out. She was able to ar-

ticulate how she felt. I remember saying to myself, whoever directed her in that retreat certainly helped her. It must have been talking it out with the director that helped her to see herself.

I think I would be correct in saying that being able to talk about our problems, helps us to face up to ourselves. Besides, the mere fact of trying to put our feelings into words clarifies our ideas in our own minds.

c. One is able to accept of one's own accord
It is very hard to explain how it happens but I know that many come through their difficulty of accepting in this way. An example may explain:

During our annual Solemn Novena to Our Lady of Perpetual Help in Clonard, Belfast, a lady met me in the church yard and said she would like to talk. This was her story: She attended the Solemn Novena faithfully each year. This year when she started she knew exactly what she wanted. Her husband was hoping for promotion in his job. Her daughter was doing an important exam. Her mother would shortly be going into hospital for tests and was frightened. These were the things she wanted God to grant her. She felt these would make her and her family happy. She had been praying for days.

Then that morning a terrible thought struck her. She realised that, when she came back from work, she was so often in bad form. She would give out to all at home that this was not done and that was not done. She complained she had to do everything in the house. She would get into black moods. There was an atmosphere in the house you could cut. It was only that morning the reality of what she was doing came home to her. She was making everyone at home miserable. Perhaps this was why her daughter rarely brought her friends home and why her husband just went silent when she was in the tantrums. The horror of what she had been doing to the family so struck her that she was amazed at how they put up with her. Then she said, 'Now I realise that those three things I was praying for were not the important things. What would make my family more happy and contented would be if I changed my selfish conduct.' Then she said, 'That is what I'm praying for now – the courage to stop giving into my selfishness.' I said to her, 'That is a special gift from God, to be able to see yourself so honestly. The courage to change is what you must pray for and work at.'

In a way, I suppose, she did not 'just think of it'. The germ of her doubt must have been smoldering away in her mind. This was merely the final step in a long process.

I feel this kind of experience brings great peace and even joy. There is the relief of giving up a futile struggle. There is the hope that now I can do something about it. I had the impression that she was joyful at having at last reached this stage. And, as a matter of fact, that has been my own personal experience. I will talk about that later.

d. Being brought to the depths

This is another well-recognised way of coming to terms with ourselves. It is a kind of shock therapy that often works. What I am describing is, of course, the classic story of the alcoholic. He keeps denying that he has a problem. He says he can stop drinking anytime he wants to. And yet he does not. He goes on and on drinking, in spite of protestations from his family and friends and loved ones. But there comes the morning he wakens up to find himself lying on the roadside, in the gutter, in his own filth and vomit. Then he begins to see what was obvious to everyone else. For the first time in his life he admits he is an alcoholic. I suppose you could say about this experience also, that it did not really happen suddenly one morning. It has been simmering away for a long time.

I imagine this is the experience of others besides alcoholics. It could be giving up smoking, or drugs or gambling. Or indeed any addiction or any weakness.

I have not asked reformed alcoholics if this is a moment of joy and relief. I imagine there would be a kind of despair at what lay before them – a life without alcohol. I remember when I eventually succeeded in giving up smoking, after years of trying, I felt uncertain about the future. Would I really be able to stay off the cigarettes? It seemed a long empty road, without the comfort of a cigarette!

e. We can use prayer to help us to acceptance
I am not referring here to asking God to help us admit our weaknesses and give us the courage to accept. We could, of course, pray for that. Rather we can use prayer to notice what is going on within ourselves. I think it can be a powerful help in this way:

When I go into pray, I may notice certain emotions bubbling up within me. I may be angry or resentful or rebellious or jealous or possessive or depressed. In the silence of prayer these feelings stand out more clearly. Now is the time to start asking myself some questions. 'Why am I reacting in this way? Why am I angry, or jealous, or possessive?' Usually I do not like to face up to these questions.

Formerly, anger, jealousy, resentment, rebellion, possessiveness, depression were not considered thoughts worthy of prayer. On the contratory, we were urged to put them aside and get back to more sublime thoughts. Now that seems to me to be foolish. First, it is not easy to get these feelings out of our mind during prayer. They will persist. Secondly, this is an opportunity to get in touch with what is really going on in us. These are the things that so preoccupy us that we do not hear the word of God. Besides, they are the very things we do not want to see and that we keep pushing into the background. Now that they have come to the fore in our consciousness, we have a God-given opportunity to have an honest look at them. For example, I could at least start by admitting that I am angry and resentful and rebellious and so on. A very good beginning indeed. I have an example of that from my own life.

Lord, I am angry
I remember on one occasion, I was asked by my superior to do a

certain job. I felt it put me in an uncomfortable, compromising position and I resented it. As a result, when I went to pray each night, I often spend most of the hour simply saying, 'I am angry, Lord. I am angry.' It took me a long time to came to terms with the situation, but I eventually did. Perhaps admitting my feelings in prayer helped me to face up to it. *Lord I am a Sinner*

St Paul prays his way into acceptance

Paul went through this process. Early in his life, he discovered in himself things he did not like. In one of his well known passages, Romans 7:14-20, he talks about this: 'I want to do what is good' and I suppose that is what we desire, at least most of the time. Yet he continues, 'But I find myself doing evil.' That is an experience we have all had. He explains it even more fully: 'I do not do the good I want to do; instead, I do the evil I do not want to do.' How often do we say, 'I do not seem to have any willpower'?

I think this difficulty of St Paul solved itself in another marvellous experience – one that gave me great hope.

Paul describes it in 2 Cor 12: He was given a vision in which he seemed to be snatched up to heaven. He received wonderful revelations that cannot be put into words. He heard things that human words may not speak. But then, as if to prevent him from being puffed up with pride, God sent him an affliction. We do not know precisely what that affliction was. Different translations describe it in different ways. The old familiar translation is, he sent me 'a sting of the flesh'. That conjures up images of impurity. Had he fallen in love with some married woman, or was it with a man, or was it persistent masturbation? On the other hand there is another translation which leads to a different interpretation. 'I was given a painful physical ailment, which acts as Satan's messenger to beat me and keep me from being proud.' This is obviously something physical. It could have been rheumatism (since he was at sea a lot). It could have been his eyesight. He may have had a weakness in the eyes. They say that when we get a big shock, it is usually the weakest part of the body that gives way. For some people it is the heart, for some it is ulcers; for Paul it was his eyes as we see on the road to Damascus. According to the *Jerome Commentary*, most scripture scholars say it was probably a physical ailment.

Whatever it was, it annoyed him very much. He tells us that 'three times I prayed to the Lord about this'. From the tone of the passage, I take it that Paul does not mean that on three occasions he made a little prayer like, 'Oh God, take this away.' I imagine he had three mighty crises. The affliction, whatever it was, so upset him that he begged earnestly for the Lord to take it away. And the Lord did not. And a second time and a third time there was another crisis and again he earnestly begged the Lord to remove it, and he did not. Then it began to dawn on Paul that the Lord was not going to remove this affliction.

And so another conclusion came to him. It did not make any difference whether he had the weakness or not. The power of the Lord was with him and now he had an added strength, that of Christ. He no longer worried about this weakness. He accepted it as part of life. He went further and accepted all the weaknesses and hardships he had to endure. He ends with a marvellous statement: 'I am content with weaknesses, insults, hardships, persecutions and difficulties for Christ's sake. For when I am weak, then I am strong' (2 Cor 12:10).

Helps to getting unstuck in anger
I suggest these as some of the things that might help us become unstuck in our anger: The kindness and acceptance of others; being able to talk about it; in some way coming to realise what the weakness is; descending to the depths like the alcoholic; becoming aware of self in prayer.

However, I think it is only when we get there and have became unstuck in our anger that we will be able to see what really worked for us. Nor will we realise immediately what an achievement this has been. It could, indeed, be a turning point. The reward that lies ahead is worth waiting for. The spiritual life

will begin to open up. Prayer enters a new phase. And all because I have been able to say, with the help of God, 'Yes, that is
me. I accept myself as I am.'

PART V

The Meeting of the Waters

CHAPTER 16

How I came to accept myself

There is a popular song in Ireland called 'The Meeting of the Waters', by Thomas Moore. Many of his poems have been set to music and are known as *Moore's Melodies*. This poem describes a beauty spot in Co Wicklow called Avoca, not far from Arklow. Here two rivers, the Avonmore and the Avonbeg meet in the Vale of Avoca.

What I am going to describe now could be called 'The Meeting of the Waters'. In the spiritual life when two things meet, something beautiful takes place. The two things are, the experience of ourselves and the experience of God.

Which of the experiences comes first? I do not know what the usual order is, but I do know that for me it was the pain of accepting myself as I am, that came first. I have no doubt that coming to accept oneself prepares the way for meeting God. Then, eventually, we can see both ourselves and God in a new way. Probably the best way of describing the experience of accepting oneself and then of meeting God would be to describe what happened to me. After all that is the only story I know personally.

Encounter with myself
In 1963 we closed the school in Ambala where I was principal. I was transferred to Bangalore which is in south India. There I was engaged full-time in giving parish missions and retreats. My superior asked me to preach a Novena to Our Lady in our own Holy Ghost Church in Bangalore. In a way, I was flattered and pleased. But, in another way, I was apprehensive. I was afraid that I would not make a success of it. Preaching before our

130

own confrères in our own churches is something we Redemptorists do not like. So I suggested to the superior to get someone else to do it. He said no, that I had to do it. So I took another tack. I suggested that two of us do it. Well, if things went wrong, I would not get all the blame! How devious we can be, or should I say, can I be? Again the answer was no. So I got down to preparing, and as usual when I have to do something, I work hard at it. I did a great deal of study and spent a long time writing my sermons.

And then the novena started. I thought it was going down well enough with the people. But then I got the feeling that some of the confrères did not like the way I was doing it. It was not what they said, but what they did not say. I found myself getting annoyed and angry. I began to defend myself in my own mind. After all, I had studied these topics more that they did! And so, 'What did they know about it?' I blamed them for their ignorance.

At that time in the religious life we had compulsory recreation, but I was free from it because I was preaching this novena. Needless to say, I did not go to recreation. I felt hurt the confrères did not give me the recognition I longed for. So I could not face them.

Then, when I went to bed at night, I could not sleep. The resentment kept running through my mind. I am sure I had failed before in my life, but this was the first time failure had this effect on me. I found it painful to accept. Me! A failure in what I thought I could do well! I was angry, blaming others, excusing myself. This went on for some time. I imagine I could have become bitter. Fortunately, I do not think I have.

After going through all that, can you imagine how I reacted the first time I read Kübler-Ross? I knew exactly what she was describing, because I had been through it. Not that I had been through physical death, as is obvious. I had gone through something similar, emotional death. Death to my cherished ideas about myself. Indeed, my experience was a classical description of Kübler-Ross's stages.

One of my difficulties with Kübler-Ross is this: When she writes of coming to acceptance, she does not give any very clear description of how this takes place. But my acceptance of this humiliating failure I remember very well. Indeed, the circumstances surrounding it are etched on my memory. And this is how it happened:

How I came ultimately to accept myself
I forget the chronology of events, but my anger and rebellion went on for some time, whether weeks or months I am not sure. It was a miserable, humiliating time. However, I remember how it resolved itself. One afternoon I had been out for a walk with another confrère. I returned to my room in the monastery. I still remember the exact room I was living in and I could bring you straight to it today. What happened then is as clear as a film playing in my mind. I opened the door and went in. I was standing inside the room and closing the door behind me, when the thought came to me, 'But they are right. I did make a mess of it. I was not as great a fellow as I had hoped.' I remember saying, even though it was before the days of popular psychology, 'That's the real me. Why try to blind myself to the truth?' A surprising thing happened. A great peace and joy descended on me. It was as if I had given up a pointless struggle and accepted the truth about myself. The weaknesses I had been so anxious to hide did not seem all that humiliating. I was now able to look my failure straight in the face. I felt a lightheartedness, a peace, a joy that to this day I cannot explain. I was now able to admit my weakness and failure to myself. That in itself was quite a victory.

However, admitting it to others was a different matter. During all that time I had been able to speak to one man only about it and he gave me great help. I do not know what I would have done without his encouragement. But it took me a long time to speak openly about it in public. No doubt I had learned a great lesson. I was very conscious of how I had come to accept my weaknesses. And I knew what a remarkable change it made in my life. So immediately after that, when I was giving retreats to religious or priests, I used say in a veiled way, 'Give up the useless struggle against the truth. Accept yourself as you are.' However, I could not go into any details about what happened to me. I felt it would have been too humiliating. My feelings were still too raw. But gradually I realised that telling others to give up the useless struggle was not as easy as that. It takes time. It is a process and a long painful process.

Looking back on it now, I see this meeting with myself as a turning point. Of course it was not a once-for-all victory over my reluctance to accept myself. True, it was a remarkable experience. But every now and again, I have to go through a like struggle. It can still be very painful. I can still feel as rejected or jealous or hurt as ever. Jealousy and hurt do not die easily. Again I am back in that feeling of darkness and despondency. Yet, since I now have some idea of what is actually happening within me, I can calm down more quickly, at least a little bit more quickly! I now try to see each occasion as God's attempt to make me a slightly better person.

Later I learned that this acceptance, standing inside my room, was not the end of the affair. A short while afterwards another event occurred which is also a landmark in my life. Indeed, it was the climax of all this period. I had an experience of God and it came out of the blue.

CHAPTER 17

An experience of God

I know now that when any of us reaches the stage of being able to admit our weaknesses and accept them, the experience of God becomes a possibility. We are on the verge. Of course I know that we cannot earn the special gifts of God. What St Paul says in Ephesians 2 is impressed indelibly on my mind: 'We are saved by faith. It is not our own doing, lest there be room for pride.' Faith, prayer, the kingdom are gratuitous, free gifts of God. Yet perhaps, just perhaps, if we remove the obstacles within ourselves, we allow God freedom to act. I look back on that failure I went through in Bangalore as very significant. Was it the fact that I ultimately accepted the painful truth about myself that made me open to the experience of God? I think it certainly had something to do with it. The experience of oneself is a gift God wants to give all of us. Jesus said, when speaking about prayer, 'Bad as you are, you know how to give good things to your children. How much more will the Father not give the Spirit to those who ask him?' (Lk 11:13) However, that gift, if it comes at all, comes in God's own time. All we can do is wait patiently, though I must admit that I was not all that patient.

Then, at last, the experience came. And when it did come it was unexpected and unlike what I had imagined. These are the details.

My experience of God

In 1963 I was giving a retreat to some nuns in a place called Quilon in Kerala. I do not recall the name of the order, but I do remember they wore a little white bonnet, the type Italian nuns often wear, with a little red cross on the front of it. A few days before the end of the retreat, I received a telegram from my

Superior, Fr Joe Breen. He was Rector of our house in Bangalore. The message read something like this: 'Proceed to Madras after retreat. Letter follows.' Immediately, I made preparations to leave. There was a train leaving Quilon for Madras at about 6.30 each morning and I arranged to go on that. But up to the time I left, the letter that was to follow did not arrive. So I did not know what I was supposed to do in Madras. However, that did not worry me unduly as I knew Madras well enough. So, early in the morning after the retreat, it was the fifteenth of August, some of the nuns came with me to the station. When the train arrived it was packed as Quilon is not a terminus. I managed to get into a second class carriage, but there were no seats free. I did the next best thing. I spread out my bedding on one of the empty berths and climbed up and lay there. I have always been a great reader and I did a lot of my reading on trains. So I was quite content stretched out on the berth, reading probably one of the latest paperback novels. And then it happened.

Unexpectedly, I had a sense of God being present. A tremendous stillness and silence descended on me. It was like being transported into another existence. I was completely absorbed and wrapped up in this sense of God being with me. And this God seemed the most wonderful person I had ever encountered. At that moment I knew with certainty that he cared for me and loved me. It seemed to me that everything in the New Testament was meant for me personally. Things like, 'If you remain in me and I remain in you, you will bear much fruit.' 'The water that I will give him will become in him a spring which will provide him with life-giving water and give him eternal life.' It was as if I were full to capacity of that life-giving water. There was a peace such as I had never experienced before. Indeed, the peace seemed to saturate me. The words from the transfiguration best described it, 'Lord, it is good for us to be here.' I was content to remain that way, absorbed in what ever it was.

Looking back on it now, it seems to have been an experience like that which St John of the Cross describes in *The Spiritual Canticle* where he talks about 'The What'. It is a realisation that one is in the presence of something, but one does not know what it is. So he calls it 'The What'. It grips and holds one enthralled. One does not want to leave and indeed it would be hard enough to do so. I have met others who have had that experience.

I thought with amazement, 'So this is what the brother in Calcutta was talking about. This is it. This is what God is like.' Though I saw nothing or heard nothing, I knew he was overwhelmingly beautiful and filling me to the full. There was a glow and a warmth and a deep contentment.

I lay there on the berth completely held by this. I had lost all interest in my book and put it aside. This was all I wanted. Hours passed. I longed for it to go on and on and it did. At some point I took out my New Testament and tried to read some. But I was still too overwhelmed to concentrate on any particular part of it. What did strike me was, 'All that is here in the New Testament took place with me in mind!' It is me he loves unto the end. It is with me he will come and make his abode. I am the beloved son in whom he is well pleased.

I knew that something extraordinary was happening. Was this what the brother had been talking about? Yet it was so different from what I had ever imagined. To be gripped and held like this was beyond anything I could have imagined.

When we came to the stations along the way, I got up and had a cup of coffee. I probably had a meal of curry and rice at Coimbatore or one of the big meal stations where the train used stop for a longer time.

When night came I slept but I recall that, in my waking moments, there was only one thought in my mind and that was God. The morning came and the sun arose at about 5.30 and the train arrived at Madras Central Station. I did not know where I would contact Fr Breen, my superior. So I headed for one of our nearest ports of call. It was the Presentation Convent at Vepery. And, sure enough, there was one of my confrères, Fr Martin

Cushnan, giving a retreat. I was still so conscious of God being present that I thought it must have been obvious to him. But of course it wasn't. He told me where Fr Breen was and I contacted him. And I continued praising God for all the wonderful things that had happened.

Was the experience valid?

But my mind was going back constantly to the experience I had on the train. I asked myself, time and time again, if it was a valid experience or if I had just imagined it. I even wondered if I was going crazy! I knew the best way to check it was to put it to some sensible person. There was a confrère who taught me in the seminary and whose room was two doors from mine. I decided to talk to him. I went to his door a number of times but turned back. I was afraid he would tell me to go off and have a bit of sense. Eventually I had courage enough to go in. I was pleasantly surprised. He took me seriously and encouraged me. I was reassured and at ease. Yes, the experience did seem to be from God. Of course the real proof would lie in how I would handle it.

CHAPTER 18

You are not far from the kingdom of God

The teacher of the law told Jesus that the most important parts of the law were to love God and to love his neighbour. Because he had given a wise answer, Jesus said to him, 'You are not far from the Kingdom of God' (Mk 12:34). I am sure Jesus says the same thing to many people.

God is constantly trying to bring us closer to him and to the kingdom. Part of the process seems to be getting us to accept ourselves as St Peter and St John the Baptist did. Then, I feel, we can hear the word of God more clearly. The kingdom of God is, indeed, near. We are open to the experience of God. If it is God's will, it may come.

But what sets us on that road is accepting ourselves. I would like to examine that theory more thoroughly now, and an example may help us to see the theory working out in practice. However, I change some of the details in this story for obvious reasons.

A sister's experience

Some years ago I was giving a retreat and a sister came to talk. She told me about her prayer. I was amazed at how deep it was. I asked her if she had ever read any of St Teresa of Avila and she said no. So I showed her a part in the *Fifth Mansion* which described what she was talking about. It was obvious she was far advanced in prayer. I asked her a question I often ask people whose prayer is deep: 'Did you have much suffering in your life?' She smiled and said, 'I am an alcoholic.' She told me afterwards that my face was a study. Surprise was written all over it. That I can understand, because I did not expect that answer. I thought she did not look the sort! But, of course, an alcoholic can be any sort of person.

I asked her that question because I have noticed down the years that anyone whose prayer is very deep has suffered a lot and, even more important, has ultimately come to accept it. Indeed, it may have taken years to come at last to an acceptance, but the length of time does not matter. To me this sister was an obvious case of that.

I asked her if I could tell her story and she told me she would be glad if it helped others.

The nun's story

I do not know how she started drinking, but eventually it became an uncontrollable habit. She had a responsible job and yet she managed to keep her drinking from others for a long time. She kept denying she was an alcoholic until her drinking became so bad, even she had to admit. She described the occasions when she was standing at the wash-basin in her room being sick and at the same time drinking from a bottle of whiskey.

She told me of the pain of having to admit she was an alcoholic. But the real suffering started when she went to an institute for alcoholics. She, a nun, had to tell her story before others. She soon discovered that alcoholics can detect dishonesty in each other and have no mercy. And so if she tried to hide anything, they knew and challenged her. It was a humiliating period. She described one day when she was going back to her convent for a break during the treatment. She was so low that she felt the urge to go into a hotel to get a drink. The urge was so strong that she was on the verge of giving in. She resisted. After she was dried out she went back to her convent and continued her work. When I heard that story I could understand why her prayer was as deep as it was.

The theory

I have noticed this so often in my work, that I take it now as a first principle: If a person has great suffering and eventually accepts it, deep prayer often follows. I want to stress that one could refuse to accept the suffering for a long time. One could keep on rebelling against the idea of seeing that weakness in oneself for years. But if, eventually, one comes to accept the suffering or the weakness, then things begin to happen. The more intense the suffering, the deeper the prayer experience. I think that is how it worked out with the sister.

It is like death and resurrection. Apparently Christ could not have had the glory of his resurrection, if he had not gone through the humiliation of the cross.

I could put it another way. An experience of self and an experience of God seem to go together. Or it could come about in the opposite way: An experience of God leads to an experience of self. There is a well known prayer of St Augustine, 'Noverim Te. Noverim Me', 'Lord, that I may know you and that I may know myself.' Knowing God and knowing myself go together. In getting to know myself, I get to know God. It is also true that in getting to know God I get to know myself. I do not know how it works but it does.

Once again I could put it in still different words. An encounter with myself is an encounter with God. Just as an encounter with God is an encounter with myself.

I see these as the two elements in conversion: an experience of myself and an experience of God. The two are always present.

How does this work out in practice?

The universal call to holiness
People often say, 'I have never met God. I have never had a deep experience of God. I would love to, but I do not seem to be that kind of person.' But just as the alcoholic could be any type of person, so there is not a certain type who encounters God. All types have had the experience. At the Second Vatican Council it was laid down as a principle that there is a universal call to holiness (Chapter 5 of *Lumen Gentium*). So it is not only the 'born' saints, like St Gerard Majella or the Curé of Ars who experience

God. There are the unexpected saints like Matt Talbot the alcoholic or the sinner like St Augustine or the prostitute like Mary Magdalen or the music-hall artiste like Eve Lavalier.

I know that encountering God is a gift that cannot be earned, nor can we achieve it by our own efforts, as St Paul says about justification. But I often wonder if the reason we do not encounter God is that we run away from encountering ourselves. As I pointed out in a previous chapter, many of us, like the nun I met in Wexford, dread the idea of having to admit the truth about ourselves. We desire a deep relationship with God and Christ, but not at that price. We feel that would be too much to bear.

This is not just a beautiful theory I have thought up. It comes from deep within my own experience, as I have tried to show. This reluctance to accept myself has been a big part of my own life. Indeed, I see it happening to me again and again. It is a never-ending struggle. Just when I have gone through a long and painful effort and seem to be accepting something I hate to see within myself, another fault or weakness comes to my notice. Then the struggle starts again. For example, there are times when things are going well enough and then a confrère makes a comment that flattens me. Or I feel an upsurge of jealousy when another is praised more than I am. Or I feel a rush of resentment, that I would be ashamed to mention to others. All this exhausts me and takes away my energy. I feel an emptiness in the pit of my stomach. I feel weary and almost unable to face the struggle again. And yet I know I still have to come to terms with that jealousy or resentment once more. It is never a once-for-all victory. I have gone through it so often before that now I have a pretty good idea of what is going on within me. And yet I am constantly surprised.

Perhaps it is because I am so aware of all this going on in myself that I am conscious of the same thing happening in the lives of others. When giving spiritual direction, I would love to say to some people, 'If only you could see what is going on in you and if you could admit it, that would change your life.' But I know from my own sensitivity that it is not as easy as that. Accepting is a whole long process, and it is painful. For example, there are things within me that I have never shared with another. There are things I just cannot voice as yet. I know exactly what some of them are, while there are others I am blind to. I may get around to them someday, but just now I seem to groan deep within me, 'Not yet, Lord, not yet!' Indeed, there are some of us who would rather die the death than admit to some of our weaknesses. Yet, until we do so we cannot come face to face with the Lord.

Why won't he accept his faults?

I know a religious who has marvellous qualities. He seems to consider that he has great judgment and taste. And usually he does things well. However, he seems temperamentally unable to admit that he is wrong, even in a small argument. But like all of us, he makes errors of judgment, or his good taste lets him down. But admit that? No. The bottom would fall out of his world. Undoubtedly, that is an uncomfortable way to live, and so he has developed a defence. Everywhere he goes he gathers a little clique around him. The little group is his support. It seems to be made up of people who will tell him what he wants to hear. They are with him constantly and seem to say nice things to him. Another part of the technique is to run the opposition down. Belittle those who do not give support. It is a pretty effective way of demolishing any opposition. I often ask myself if this is the bulwark he has erected to keep away the things he cannot face. Some day that bulwark may give way and it will be like a dam bursting. I feel that someone like that must find it mighty hard to admit to any chinks in his armour.

Why can't we take the plunge?

I would love to say to him, 'If only you could take the plunge.' For all of us, if only we could face up to that one thing, that one problem, accept that one humiliating trait of character, we would be through to the Lord. But here is the problem. In our hearts we are saying 'No Lord, not that. That would be just too much. Anything but that.' Or we say, with St Augustine, 'Not yet Lord, but later.'

To accept that weakness, painful though it is, seems to me to be the breakthrough. That is the point at which things begins to happen in our spiritual life: when I admit my weaknesses and try to accept them.

I say this to myself, just as I say it to others: 'Take the plunge. Admit it. Brace yourself for the pain.' And behold the heavens open! You are not far from the kingdom of God.

CHAPTER 19

A new kind of life

When I arrived at Madras Central on that day in August 1963, I was still in a daze after the experience of the day and the night in the train. God still seemed to be present. But I quickly realised that life had to go on. I contacted my superior and learned that he wanted me to give a retreat to the Franciscan Missionaries of Mary in Mylapore.

My itinerary after that becomes vague. I got back to Bangalore eventually. After the bustle and involvement of giving retreats and rushing for trains, the peace was unbelievable. And the presence of God was still there. Indeed, it was pretty constant. Often when I was walking along the corridor I knew God was with me. When I went to bed at night, my last thought was God. If I woke up in the middle of the night, I thought immediately of God. On waking in the morning, my first thought was God. That was the idyllic period of my life. Camelot was in Bangalore or wherever I was travelling.

My new life begins
I was given something new by God. It was like a new beginning, or re-entering the religious life again. It was like entering marriage, to use John of the Cross's language. I could not possibly foresee what lay ahead. However, it was not a few days' wonder. Nor was it a mere a flash in the pan, as had often happened me before. Anything but. The experience stayed with me for a number of years. This was a new way of living, a new way of being. What a contrast it was from my life before.

My former life

I see, now, that before I met that Christian Brother in Calcutta, there was very little of God in my life. He was in the background. I said few enough prayers, and then reluctantly. Prayer was not a priority. By and large the things of God left me cold. Other things absorbed me, principally my work. Then there were my pastimes. At one time I loved going out to parties. And in some places in India, the people were only too glad to invite us. Films I have always loved, even since I was a youngster growing up in Belfast. I still love them and get a thrill out of going. In India they were one of the few pieces of entertainment we had. I remember that in Bombay going to a film was a big night out. It is the same with reading. I have always been a great reader. There was one of the confrères in India who used come to me when he wanted a good book. I was always well up in the latest novels!

Though I was not God-orientated, I was a fairly efficient missioner and retreat giver. I worked hard, because I am made that way. I enjoyed travelling around, especially in India which is a fascinating country. There was a certain thrill in going to new places. I felt like Stanley and Livingstone, conquering new territories! Besides, I loved the excitement of big missions in cities like Bombay or Madras or Delhi. There was great variety in visiting the homes in different parts of the country. Above all I loved the applause that followed a good sermon.

I see now, that all this enthusiastic work was going on in spite of the fact that there was little of God in my life. That still amazes me. I often look back on it, and say cynically, 'Prayer must not be all that important. Wasn't the work successful enough? After all, there was no thunderbolt from heaven!' And yet I am forced to ask myself, what effect the work had on people. I am sure they saw through it. I feel that, after all the work, there may not have been a ripple left when it was over.

A new element in my life

And then these experiences changed all that. A pattern began to form in my life. I can trace the stages of the process I mentioned before. As usual, I was kept very busy with missions and retreats. I did them all with a new zest. But other new elements entered my life. I read the scriptures. I spent hours in prayer. If I were in my room, studying or reading or praying, I wanted to go to the oratory. There was a deep longing for prayer. But if I went to the oratory I felt guilty that I was not doing my work. However, when travelling on trains or buses, my delight was to read the scriptures and spend hours in prayer.

Meeting God in a new way

And God was still present to me. I was more often aware of him than I had ever been. I suppose I was gradually getting to know more about God and Jesus, and that became a passion with me. This was the time I discovered the spiritual classics and there were plenty of them in our library. I read those I mentioned before: Poulain, Lehodey and Chapman. It was not a mere browsing through them. I studied them. I went back to Marmion, whom we had read as students. I did not yet get fully into John of the Cross and Teresa of Avila. That was to follow later. I just dabbled in them at the time. A great find was a little book of extracts from the writings of John of the Cross, by a Fr Steward, SJ. That I carried around with me. However, there were few good modern books on contemplation. At that time, contemplation was still looked on with suspicion. I did not talk about it openly. Even on retreats to religious when I spoke a lot about prayer, I never used the word contemplation. Nor did I talk in detail of my own experiences. I made veiled references. One did not bare one's soul in those days. That would have been showing off. Certainly one did not admit one's faults in public! Even more so, my feelings were still too raw, especially about my weaknesses.

So my work continued as usual. For over a year I was still stationed in Bangalore. Most of my time was taken up with giving parish missions and retreats. That meant I spent a lot of time on trains. The railway system was one of the great things the British left in India, thousands of miles of it. Most of us Redemptorists travelled quite a few of those miles!

Another memorable train journey
One image of that time remains with me. It sums up my life at
that time. When I was travelling on trains alone, I used spend
hours in prayer, since the journeys often lasted a day and a
night. One day in particular I recall in detail. It was the Sunday
after President Kennedy was shot, and that was 24 November
1963. I was travelling to Secunderabad to preach a retreat to the
Little Sisters of the Poor. I got on the train in Bangalore early in
the morning. At first there was a big scramble to get newspapers
to read the latest on the assassination. The news stunned India
as much as the rest of the world. Newspapers were hard to get.
However, the papers that were in the carriage were being
passed from hand to hand. Indians are friendly and generous in
that way. When things calmed down, I remember taking out
that little book with extracts from St John of the Cross. I was
wrapped up all day reading it and praying. I remember as the
sun went down in the west, God seemed so close. Praying like
that became part of my life at that time. I was very much a con-
templative and a little bit of a hermit!

I realise now that there could be a danger of our gloating over
our experience of God and hugging it to ourselves. We could
live in our own little world telling ourselves that we were different and better than others. This was our big secret. Perhaps I
thought like that at one time, until I saw how prodigal God is of
his gifts. He has given similar gifts to so many. I saw that in the
many people who spoke to me on missions and retreats.

An important lesson I learned was this: The talents God gives us
are not meant to be wrapped in a napkin and buried for safe-
keeping. They are for others and for the Church. I only hope my
apostolic work kept my two feet on the ground and among the
people of God.

There were two big influences in my life at that time. Each
brought about its own changes.

A new Pentecost

My attitude towards my work changed for another reason. Did you notice the time I am talking about? It was the 1960s. For me they were glorious years. In other words, all these things were happening to me against the back-drop of the Second Vatican Council. The calling of the Council by Pope John XXIII took all of us by surprise. I remember the feeling of expectation and excitement. A number of us read the book by Hans Küng, *The Council and Reunion*. It was written to prepare the church for the coming Council. Two points I remember from it: we are a church of sinners; and the Church is in constant need of reform. Believe it or not, those were new ideas at the time.

Vatican II

Then the Council opened on 11 October 1962, with great fanfare. We eagerly awaited news from Rome. It must have been a great time for journalists. All the papers, both Catholic and secular, gave a lot of coverage. Even the Indian dailies, which were in no way Christian, seemed to consider the Council important. Then there was a news-sheet that came to us from the Franciscans in Pakistan. All these were full of the latest gossip about different personalities like Octaviani and Suenens and Agaganian. Octaviani was the big bad man – quite unfairly, I imagine. I loved it all and read avidly what I could lay my hands on.

Then the documents, promulgated by the Council, began to arrive, often in bad translations. The ones I read most eagerly were *Lumen Gentium, Gaudeum et Spes* and *Perfectae Caritatis*. I remember trying to study them, even though we had no commentaries, which only appeared much later. But the document that had an immediate effect was the *Constitution on Sacred Liturgy*. Before long we were saying Mass facing the people and in the vernacular. There was the same conservative opposition to the changes as in other parts of the world. I gave a mission in a certain parish where there were statues of all sizes in every nook and cranny in the sacristy, the hall and the priest's house. Later I heard the story. A small number of the parishoners were opposed to changing the big Portugese altar, with about fifty statues. One Saturday night the parish priest had the statues removed and got a team of carpenters to take down the big wooden altar. The people arrived on Sunday morning to find a small altar facing them.

Vatican II and the apostolate

They were heady times. We Redemptorists in India had many good seminars on scripture and the liturgy. We felt we had a new vision of the church and the Mass and community. I remember trying to absorb all that, because I felt the Holy Spirit was speaking to us. Then there was the challenge of implementing the vision. That would not be easy. I realised that our preaching and our work in general would never be quite the same again. Of course, that upset a few of our confrères who were opposed to any change. However, I welcomed it all because I felt it was needed in the church. There was a parish priest in Bombay for whom we frequently preached. He used say to me that the dust of Vatican II would settle down soon. I told him I would do my best to keep it airborne.

Many of us struggled to grasp that vision and put it into words. Writing new sermons was a must. I remember on one occasion, when I was in Bombay, going off with my typewriter and the Vatican II documents to a convent in Andheri. I wanted peace and quiet to do some writing. I eventually wrote sermons on the church, the Mass and community. And I used them often down the years.

Constant work

All of us were on the go all the time, and so the amount of apostolic work I did at that time seemed to increase. I was out constantly giving parish missions and retreats. I went as far as West Pakistan and Ceylon, as they were then called. I did work in many parts of India, from the north to the south. Sometimes I was with other fathers, sometimes alone. I loved it all because I was young and healthy and keen on travel.

Struggles against weaknesses

However, it would be unreal to give the impression that life was all joy. I can remember some hard belts, some from confrères, some from superiors. That was the time superiors acted as if they were superior! I still remember a few things that really hurt. Besides I had a constant struggle against my own weaknesses. From a few entries in my diaries I detect a continual stream of little annoyances, and disappointments and hurts and jealousies that I had to accept. No doubt they caused me pain at the time, yet the interesting thing is that if I had not made those entries, I would not remember any of those incidents. In recent diaries I find the same thing – hurts mentioned and not one memory left of them. I suppose in a way it is good to be able to forget. Of course we also forget the hurts we caused others. People have reminded me of hurts I caused them and yet I have no memory of them. That I regret.

The scene began to change

The second big influence on my life at that time happened in November 1964. I was appointed Rector of our house at Chembur in Bombay. It came out of the blue. It was just after the Eucharistic Congress in Bombay, a mighty event for the Catholics of India. Pope Paul VI attended. Unfortunately some of us had to miss it, as a number of retreats had to be given elsewhere. I was giving a retreat to the girls in the Presentation Convent, Church Park, Madras. I got a phone call from Fr Jim Connolly. He told me he had been appointed Vice-Provincial and that I was the new Rector of our house in Bombay. I was stunned. I felt I was not the sort who became a superior. I remember going to Bombay with a feeling of impending doom, because I had just witnessed a Rector getting a terrible time. When I arrived in Bombay I told someone I felt I was being thrown to the lions. Actually it was not that bad. It worked out well enough.

But being rector meant that my work increased. We had a fairly big parish. There was a mighty boys' school, and we had a mission team that was in great demand. I had a lot more to do.

Besides running the house, I had to arrange all the missions and retreats for the community. I was out pretty constantly on work. When I was at home, house affairs kept me occupied. The work of administration began to occupy me more and more.

I was rector there for two terms, which worked out at nearly six years.

More administration

Then in 1969 the work became even more burdensome. I was elected Vice-Provincial of our Indian Vice-Province. It meant really being provincial as we were practically autonomous. And, of course, my preoccupations increased. I was on the move frequently, visiting the twelve houses we had in India, both north and south and the two in Sri Lanka.

A big problem began to emerge during my term. After visiting all the houses and talking to each confrère, I came to the conclusion that the time was ripe for us to become an independent Province. We were still under the Irish Province in some matters. Besides, we never had an Indian Provincial. I had often heard older Redemptorists talking about how the Irish felt when we were still part of the English Province. No doubt many Indians felt the same way. I understood their feelings only too well, so with my Consultors, I started the process of our becoming a separate province. It was going into the unknown and a lot of discussion and persuading had to be done. I had to make a visit to Ireland for a Chapter and visited Rome on the way. Eventually it was decided in Rome and in Dublin that India and Ceylon should be a separate province. Many of us were determined that an Indian Provincial should be elected. It turned out that way and Fr Bernard Pereira was elected.

Where was my prayer life?

Just recalling all those years in Bombay and Bangalore, nine altogether, makes me exhausted! Where did all of us get the energy? They were marvellous, hectic years. And it was a happy time working with so many of the confrères, Indian and Irish. But my prayer life took an awful battering. I was faithful enough for a few years when I went to Bombay first and did indeed keep it up. But the extra work, the constant travelling around, the frequent partying all began to take their toll. But I will not blame the work. I had become careless. The vision had dimmed. The Lord had given me a talent and I had not handled it well. Other things became more interesting. Again God faded into the background. Yet deep prayer still remained the ideal for me. I wanted to get back to where I had been, but I didn't. So I used feel guilty, and still do. Of course, it was not the job that caused it. I am sure that others in my situation could have kept up a good prayer life.

CHAPTER 20

The Lord returns

I returned to Ireland in 1972. After nine years of active administration, the spark from heaven did not shine as brightly as before. What the future held for me, I did not know. I presumed I would return to India after the usual year at home, but it did not turn out that way. I was scarcely home, staying with my mother in Belfast, when I had a phone call from our Irish Provincial, Fr Jim McGrath. He asked me if would be Rector of our house in Dublin, Marianella. I had not much choice but to accept, so that decided my future. My marvellous adventure in India was over. I was really working on the Irish scene for the first time as a priest.

So there I was, into administration again. I was kept very busy. Besides being Rector of a community of up to fifty Redemptorists, I was in charge of the mission team. I took all this as a new challenge.

The apostolate in Ireland

I found that there was a tremendous search going on among Irish Redemptorists. They were trying to devise a new form of the parish mission, in an attempt to get across the ideas of Vatican II. Eventually a new type of mission evolved. I have great admiration for those who devised it. Since I was in charge of the mission team in Dublin I was much involved. We did many big parish missions in Dublin and in the adjacent dioceses. We were on the go pretty well all the time. It was my job to arrange these missions, just as it had been in Bombay. That meant frequent visits to the parish clergy before we went out on the mission. Then during the summer I gave retreats to religious. I was back again into a life of activity.

The dissatisfaction returns

You can imagine the disastrous effect that constant activity had on my prayer life. The decline had already started half way through my six years in Bombay. I was even more preoccupied when I was Vice-Provincial. It was no better when I was Rector in Marianella. Deep prayer had practically gone. True, I was always present at the morning office and other community prayers during the day. I said Mass each day and got in a few bits and pieces. That I would consider the bare minimum. I suppose my heart was not really in it.

Eventually I began to yearn to get back to prayer again. With the Charismatic movement beginning to catch on, there was a growing atmosphere of prayer around. I never got involved in the actual movement, but I did feel the Lord was prodding me. Though I did not realise it at the time, I was back to the beginning of the process again as in the early 60s. I can look back now and see myself going through the same stages as before. The dissatisfaction with my life returned. Once again, I knew there had to be something more to the Christian and religious life than the way I was living it.

The fervour of lay people began to amaze me. Prayer groups were being formed all over the country. To spend long periods in prayer was becoming fashionable. Books on prayer began to appear, even on deep prayer and contemplation. All that increased my dissatisfaction. And true enough, before long the catalyst appeared.

The catalyst

The spark from heaven did fall. We Redemptorists had a mission seminar in our Retreat House in Limerick. The seminar itself was not memorable, but what followed it was, at least for me. When the seminar was over, about twenty-five of us stayed on in the Retreat House for a retreat. That was the first common retreat for Redemptorists I experienced in Ireland. The emphasis during the retreat was on two things, Charismatic prayer and centring prayer. I have never been all that interested in

Charismatic prayer, but the other prayer, yes. It was what I had been used to. During the retreat, we had many sessions of praying together in stillness. And now for the first time in years, I found myself getting immersed in prayer. I do not remember how long the retreat was, but by the end of it I was beginning to pray as formerly. I now look back on that retreat as the catalyst.

When I got back to Marianella, I tried to spend more time in prayer. There was a small empty room at the top of the house. I got it decorated and used it as a prayer room.

Again I began to see things anew

All the things that happened to me years before seemed to happen again. I began to see God and Jesus in a new way. I could feel their presence in prayer. I was back again to reading the scriptures. And I certainly began to see myself in a new way. My faults became more obvious and that is easy to understand. One thing I had been trying to do for years was to stop smoking. I was a heavy, heavy smoker and I knew I just had to stop. Others used tell me I was a disgrace! At last, after much effort, I managed to give it up.

Once again, prayer became interesting. When giving retreats I talked more about prayer. I even talked openly about contemplation, because so many people were interested in it. I wrote new conferences on prayer. I found that a good way of praying during retreats to religious was to join them in a holy hour each evening. To me, praying with other people, in this way, is a completely different experience from praying alone. Besides, it meant that no matter how busy I was during the retreat, I always had at least an hour of prayer. Indeed, the prayer experience on retreats used to encourage me to go to the little prayer room or the chapel when I returned to Marianella. Gradually prayer became part of my life. I was back to where I had been before.

I am sure there are many like me who have fallen away from prayer. Perhaps they feel that same dissatisfaction. Their lives may be uninteresting and boring. I just say to them, try to get back to prayer. Keep at it and it will come.

I get the sack!

After six years as Rector in Marianella, I got the sack. I went to our country house in Esker, Co Galway. After fifteen consecutive years in administration, it was a great relief to be off. At last I had peace and quiet. I was on the mission staff in Esker and we were kept busy. However, between missions and retreats, I had more time for prayer and reading. The Lord seemed to be guiding me in two events that helped me very much.

I studied John of the Cross

I got myself a copy of the latest translation of the *Collected Works of St John of the Cross* by Kavanaugh and Rodrigues. I had been studying John intermittantly. But now I got down to going through his writings from beginning to end. Gradually I got a clearer picture of his whole theory. John is not easy reading, but what kept me going was the fact that I recognized so much of what he described in my own experiences. I grew to love his writings. With some parts I have just a nodding acquaintance, other parts I know almost by heart. I began, too, reading St Teresa of Avila in the new translation by the same translators. What I concentrated on were the well-known sections where she talks of the development of prayer. All those, at least, I know well. John and Teresa were my inspiration.

A course on spirituality

Another event helped me a lot. In 1978, I did a course on Spiritual Direction in Manresa House, the Jesuit house in Dublin. We had to attend for a weekend once a month for a year. Part of the course was that we had to make a directed retreat of six days and another of thirty days. This was to let us experience being directed, before we would be let loose on directing others. The course certainly got me back into prayer in a big way. Part of each weekend was spent in prayer and sharing with the group on how our prayer went. When I saw how my companions prayed, it encouraged me.

Then, towards the end of the course, each of us had to write a paper on some aspect of spirituality. I chose the doctrine of St

John of the Cross. I got down to reading John more deeply. I remember being up until two and three in the morning getting the paper finished in time. I do not think it was a great paper, but I learned a lot more about John of the Cross.

Directed retreats

The high lights of the course for me were the six-day and the thirty-day retreats. During the six-day, which was in January 1979, I began again to have deep experiences of prayer. I suppose it was the prayerful atmosphere that helped. But my prayer went even deeper during the thirty days, which we did in Tabor House, Milltown, Dublin. This really got me back to those days of prayer before I was involved in administration.

A frequent experience during the thirty days was at prayer each night. Most of us doing the retreat would gather in the chapel, sitting on the ground, propped up on cushions. I can remember often beginning my prayer surrounded by about twenty other priests and nuns. I would try my best to get into stillness. And then, before I knew, I would come to and find myself alone in the chapel! Often more than an hour had passed. What used to amaze me was that I had not heard the sound of anyone leaving. Yet I knew with absolute certainty that I had not been asleep. That happened quite often during the thirty days. I was somewhat uneasy, until I studied again this phenomenon in both John of the Cross and Teresa

But the joyful prayer experience was only one side. There was also the painful part. I found I had the same reluctance to accept the weaknesses that surfaced during the thirty days retreat. At times, when I had to face some weakness, I was angry and rebellious. I remember one day walking the streets of Clonskeagh, boiling with anger at some fault my director pointed out to me.

When the year's course was over I started to put spiritual direction into practice. So for years, besides many missions, I have been giving retreats to religious, both preached and directed. As you can imagine, all this has gradually given me a sense of purpose in life.

So that is the journey! It really started for me in the 1960s. I often think back to those days in the school in Ambala. In spite of the feelings of dissatisfaction, I knew that there had to be something more in life. Then when things did happen, they were beyond what I had ever imagined. Unfortunately, I did not handle that talent very well.

To have received those graces and lived according to them for sometime and then to have given up as I did, that I regret.

However, the fact that God welcomed me a second time amazes me. That helps me to understand what St Peter must have felt. At the last supper, Peter said, 'I will never leave you, even though all the rest do.' And we all know what happened. He knew immediately the enormity of what he had done, 'and he broke down and cried' (Mk 15:69-72). I have some idea of how Peter felt. I did the same as he did. He was forgiven and went on to great things.

I am grateful, too, that the process started for me again. I could easily have given up altogether. And I think life would have been very empty if I had continued living as I was.

I thank God for leading me along the path he did. Not only do I thank him for the joyful things, I thank also him for the painful things. I would hate to go through some of those trials again. However, I am glad now that I did because they may have made me a slightly better person. Now that I am on the second round, I hope I will be able to persevere and keep in touch with the Lord.

Yet it is only now, after the event, that I have some idea where he has been leading me in the past. I wonder what more he has in store for me. But I realise that he loves me for nothing. He loves me just as I am. I know, too, that he is welcoming me forward and that his welcome is transforming. A second time he was waiting for me. After all, he is a God of welcomes.